"In an article written in 2006 for *Christianity Today*, Collin Hansen gave us a framework to understand the contemporary revival of Reformed theology—something so many felt was happening but so few could describe. Now he invites us to journey with him on a voyage of discovery as he travels the nation, learning how our restless youth are discovering anew the great doctrines of the Christian faith. Weary of churches that seek to entertain rather than teach, longing after the true meat of the Word, these young people are pursuing doctrine and are fast becoming new Calvinists. With a keen eye for detail, descriptive analysis, and a strong grasp of theology, Hansen shows where this movement originated, tells who has become involved, and suggests where it may be leading. Any Christian will benefit from reading this book and discovering how God is moving among the young, the restless, and the Reformed."

—TIM CHALLIES, author, *The Discipline of Spiritual Discernment*; blogger at Challies.com

"*Young, Restless, Reformed* is the product of some outstanding research by Collin Hansen. Regardless of one's theological persuasion, this book will help the reader gain valuable insight into the growing Reformed movement in America."

—JERRY BRIDGES, author of *The Pursuit of Holiness*

"If you think doctrine—particularly the Calvinist kind—is a mere head-trip that undermines evangelism and saps devotion, you need to read *Young, Restless, Reformed*. In his journalistic travels, Collin Hansen has uncovered a fresh movement of young Christians for whom doctrine—particularly the Calvinist kind—fuels evangelism, kindles passion, and transforms lives. Read it and rejoice."

—DAVID NEFF, Editor-in-Chief, Christianity Today media group

"While other movements have been making a bigger splash in the headlines, a number of strategic ministries have been quietly (and sometimes not so quietly!) upholding the doctrines of grace, planting churches, seeing people converted, teaching the whole counsel of God. These are now beginning to coalesce in a variety of mutually encouraging ways. It is a pleasure to recommend Collin Hansen's survey of some of these movements. This is not the time for Reformed triumphalism. It is the time for quiet gratitude to God and earnest intercessory prayer, with tears, that what has begun well will flourish beyond all human expectation."

—D. A. CARSON, Research Professor of New Testament, Trinity Evangelical Divinity School

"Calvinism is more popular today among evangelicals—especially young Americans—than it has been in nearly two centuries. This lively account of its resurgence from an up-and-coming partisan is must reading for ministry leaders working with young adults. There is much that older Christians can do to help the young and restless to mature in Christian discipleship and witness. I pray that Hansen's book will function, then, as more than a handy digest of the latest trend in our (endlessly trendy) evangelical movement. It is a wake-up call to baby boomers to move beyond the superficial faith they taught their children and to grow with them in the knowledge and love of God."

—Douglas A. Sweeney, Associate Professor of Church History, Trinity Evangelical Divinity School

Young, Restless, Reformed

A JOURNALIST'S JOURNEY WITH THE NEW CALVINISTS

COLLIN HANSEN

CROSSWAY BOOKS

WHEATON, ILLINOIS

Library of Congress Cataloging-in-Publication Data
Hansen, Collin, 1981–
 Young, restless, reformed : a journalist's journey with the new Calvinists / Collin Hansen.
  p. cm.
 Includes bibliographical references and index.
 ISBN 978-1-58134-940-5 (tpb)
 1. Calvinsm. 2. Calvinsim—History—20th century. 3. Reformed Church—History—20th century. 4. Calvinists. I. Title.
BX9422.3.H37 2008
284'.273090511—dc22   2008006501

VP		17	16	15	14	13	12	11	10	09	08
15	14	13	12	11	10	9	8	7	6	5	4	3	2	1

To

LAUREN

called according to God's purpose,
lovely, patient, and kind,
precious in his sight

Contents

Acknowledgments

I owe a great deal to so many who made this book possible. Thanks especially to the subjects of this book, who eagerly opened their lives to me. I appreciate Justin Taylor, who consulted with me throughout the writing process and significantly shaped the final draft. Zack Boren, a devoted friend and perceptive reader, helped me understand what worked and what did not. I am in debt to my *Christianity Today* colleagues, who enabled this reporting by allowing me to travel and pursue my interests. Thanks in particular to Stan Guthrie, whose advice is better than gold.

I can always count on my parents, Randy and Julie, for encouragement. They have long modeled self-sacrificial love and now reflect the power of God's irresistible grace.

Lauren, you are the love of my life, my best friend and first reader. By God's grace, he makes our love unconditional.

Above all I thank the God who found nothing good in me but saved me nonetheless. To Father, Son, and Holy Spirit be all honor and glory, now and forever.

Collin Hansen

Prologue

Near the beginning of my tenure at *Christianity Today*, the emerging church was all the rage. Editors tended to view this youthful stirring with appropriate skepticism, wondering about the implications of tweaking theology to reach postmodern cultures. Still, emerging leaders such as Brian McLaren built audiences with provocative critiques of modern evangelicalism. After all, emerging Christians are not the only ones who worry that today's church has relaxed standards for holiness and disconnected itself from history. In November 2004 we published a cover story by Andy Crouch, who introduced "The Emergent Mystique." But he did not make many friends within this ill-defined segment when he observed common traits among emerging Christians, such as their careful care for cool hair.

The talk about emerging Christians put me in a difficult spot. As the youngest *CT* editor, I should have known more about this up-and-coming group. On the contrary, I didn't know anyone who was emerging, even though my friends and I had recently experienced the fruits of postmodern relativism in college. We had witnessed the complete breakdown of moral authority and heard apathetic responses to Christian truth claims when we shared from the *Four Spiritual Laws* booklet. Yet we viewed these reactions not as problems with Christianity but as problems with sinners who reject God's grace shown through Jesus Christ.

After one staff discussion about the emerging church, I talked about these experiences with my boss at *CT*. I expressed concern that when *Christianity Today* reports about the emerging church, we might give the impression that this group will become the next wave in evangelicalism. If anything, in my limited sphere I saw a return to traditional Reformed theology. My friends read John Piper's book *Desiring*

God and learned from Wayne Grudem's *Systematic Theology*. They wanted to study at the Southern Baptist Theological Seminary and sent each other e-mails when they saw good sales for the five-volume set of Charles Spurgeon sermons.

Maybe that was just our little clique in Campus Crusade for Christ at Northwestern University. Or was it? I started thinking about leading seminaries in the United States and noticed a number of Calvinists in leadership positions. I considered millions of books sold by Piper and his yearly appearances at the popular Passion conference. Yale University Press had just released a major biography of Jonathan Edwards. Reformed theology had recently become a major point of contention in the nation's largest Protestant body, the Southern Baptist Convention. Maybe it wasn't just our group.

So I embarked on a nearly two-year journey to discover whether my experiences had been unique or a sign of something bigger. In locales as diverse as Birmingham, Alabama, and New Haven, Connecticut, I sought to find out what makes today's young evangelicals tick. The result should help us learn what tomorrow's church might look like when they become pastors or professors. Even today, common threads in their diverse testimonies will tell the story of God's work in this world.

CHAPTER ONE

Born Again Again

PASSION CONFERENCE
ATLANTA, GEORGIA

Downtown Atlanta was prepared to host the 1996 Summer Olympics. But I don't know if any city is prepared to accommodate nearly twenty-three thousand college students all trying to check into their hotels at the same time. At least not when they show up New Year's Day less than twenty-four hours after the home-state football team won a bowl game in Atlanta's Georgia Dome.

Daunting lines at the Sheraton Hotel ruined my best-laid plans to arrive on time for the opening session of the 2007 Passion conference. The downstairs lobby teemed with college students knitting, chatting, or listening to iPods as they waited in lines that did not move. After a few minutes of moping and fruitless scheming, I determined to make the best of a bad situation. Suddenly the insufferable lines appeared differently—*a captive interview audience*, I thought.

Soon I overheard two young men in the line next to me talking about theology and church. There is no tactful way to butt in on some-one else's conversation. So I just asked why they signed up for Passion. The older man said he escorted a group of college students from Florida Hospital Church, a Seventh-day Adventist congregation in Orlando. Among them was Robin Treto, eighteen, a freshman at Seminole Community College. "I'm a John Piper fiend," Robin responded. He spoke excitedly, yet with careful thought for his words.

"He's so Jesus-centered in his preaching," Robin said of Piper. "He doesn't just share anecdotal stories. I look to guys like Piper because he looks to Jesus."

Piper, the best-selling author and pastor for preaching at Bethlehem Baptist Church in Minneapolis, Minnesota, is a Passion fixture. His book *Don't Waste Your Life* emerged from a talk he delivered in front of about forty thousand students for the Passion OneDay event in 2000. But what exactly is a John Piper fiend? Robin apparently listened online to two hundred Piper sermons from the book of Romans alone during just four months. That's a John Piper fiend.

I was curious to learn from Robin how an Adventist student from Florida became such a big fan of a Baptist pastor in Minnesota. Seventh-day Adventists have sometimes worshiped at arm's length from the evangelical mainstream. Robin began to explain that he has only believed in Jesus Christ for a couple of years. Just a few months earlier, Robin would not have been confused by anyone for the type who sits down and listens to hundreds of sermons. Between smoking marijuana and heavy alcohol use, Robin had rebelled against what he described as the legalistic environment at the Adventist church of his parents, who had emigrated from Cuba.

Robin's lifestyle began to change when he was sixteen. The older cousin who introduced him to party life began talking about Jesus. His cousin had been touched by the gospel. Sitting together at his cousin's house, they opened the Bible and read Romans 8 together. Robin was so impressed by the dramatic and unexpected conversion that he patiently heard his cousin out. But the Bible did not make sense to him. Frustrated, Robin left his cousin's house confused. Yet as he sat in his car and prepared to drive away, everything suddenly changed. The words of Scripture began to strike him as true. He understood at once that Jesus Christ had paid the penalty on the cross for his sins and three days later rose from the dead, achieving salvation for those who would believe. In a moment Robin lost his heart for partying but gained a new heart filled with passion for God.

"That's why I have hope for a generation like ours," Robin told me. "The gospel is powerful enough to change hearts."

Robin did not return to his parents' church. But he did not leave Adventism. Shortly after Robin's conversion, a pastor from a nearby Adventist church gave him CDs with conference talks from C. J. Mahaney, a charismatic teacher from suburban Maryland. Mahaney delivered the messages over the span of six years at the New Attitude conference, launched by pastor/author Joshua Harris for young adults. Robin also listened to some of Harris's talks. During one message, Harris quoted Piper's manifesto, *Desiring God*. This stirring call to "Christian hedonism" argues that "God is most glorified in us when we are most satisfied in him."[1] Piper's teaching about Calvinism squared with Robin's growing knowledge of Scripture.

You will find no explanation and no index entry for Calvinism in *Desiring God*. But it's all there, if you know what to look for. Calvinists—like their namesake, Reformation theologian John Calvin—stress that the initiative, sovereignty, and power of God is the only sure hope for sinful, fickle, and morally weak human beings. Furthermore, they teach that the glory of God is the ultimate theme of preaching and the focus of worship.

Many recognize Calvinism, described by some as Reformed theology, by the acronym TULIP.[2] You won't find these terms in *Desiring God* either. But you will find the concepts as early as the second chapter. Piper quotes Romans 3:10—"None is righteous, no, not one" (**T**otal depravity). A little later Piper writes, "Regeneration is totally unconditional. It is owing solely to the free grace of God. 'It does not depend on the one who wills or runs, but on God who has mercy' (Romans 9:16). We get no credit. He gets all the glory."[3] Here you can see **U**nconditional election and a hint of **I**rresistible grace. Piper explains **L**imited atonement in a footnote. "All contempt for [God's] glory is duly punished, either on the Cross, where the wrath of God is propitiated for those who believe, or in hell, where the wrath of God is poured out on those who don't."[4] In a later footnote Piper defends eternal security, or **P**erseverance of the saints, from Romans 8:30—"And those whom [God] predestined he also called, and those whom he called he also justified, and those whom he justified he also glorified."[5]

These beliefs didn't go down easy with Robin. He described Calvinism as rough sledding at first. God's sovereignty was a fear-

---

[1]John Piper, *Desiring God* (Sisters, OR: Multnomah, 1996), 238.
[2]For a fuller explanation, see Chapter Two of this book, "Out of Bethlehem."
[3]Piper, *Desiring God*, 64.
[4]Ibid., 296.
[5]Ibid., 302.

some concept. But these fears evaporated as he saw the scriptural basis through positive presentations.

"Guys who taught it to me—Mahaney, Harris, Piper—said it humbly and so passionately," Robin explained. "They loved what they were talking about."

I asked Robin how Calvinism meshes with the Adventist church he attends. "It doesn't," Robin answered. He spent his first semester of college studying theology at Southern Adventist University in Tennessee. His increasing unwillingness to go along with unique points of Adventist theology led to conflict with faculty. He returned home to Orlando rather than cementing an unwanted reputation as the only non-Adventist theology major.

But if he's not Adventist, why does Robin still attend an Adventist church? Because that's where he can make a difference and maybe even teach others with his Calvinist theology. Besides, since Adventists meet on Saturdays, he can spend his Sunday mornings in Saint Andrew's Chapel in Sanford, Florida, where R. C. Sproul preaches. He first heard about the famed Calvinist teacher when he read Sproul's classic *The Holiness of God*. He was thrilled to learn that Sproul, a Presbyterian, preaches in the Orlando area. Robin considers Sproul to be the best Bible teacher in town. "But I skip the first thirty minutes," Robin clarified. He arrives just in time to miss the traditional music but still catch the sermon. That's no surprise. Sproul doesn't exactly share a taste for the modern praise music that unites the college students at Passion.

"We wait all year to worship like this," Robin said of Passion.

If Calvinism finds renewed interest among the young, you cannot understand that resurgence without understanding Passion. Not that Passion proclaims Calvinism by name. Piper doesn't know what Passion founder Louie Giglio believes about Reformed theology. But he does know that Giglio adores the glory of God and desires to spread God's renown around the world. And Giglio doesn't protest what Piper teaches the students. That's good enough for Piper.

"I'm sixty. What am I doing at Passion?" Piper asked when we met at his home. Unlike Giglio, an athletic man who wears tight-fitting, hip T-shirts, nothing in Piper's appearance or dress would indicate popularity among youth. Though obviously fit and healthy, Piper does not cut a strong physical presence. Unlike his dynamic, intense preaching style, he spoke to me in a friendly, calm manner. But do not mistake friendly with jovial. Talking for about two hours over dinner, he spoke with quiet seriousness. He looks like a college professor with tousled thin hair and glasses. Actually, he did teach at Bethel College (now university) in Minnesota until 1980 when he moved to Bethlehem Baptist Church.

Piper may not know what he's doing at Passion, but it's obvious to students such as Robin why he fits with Passion. Piper lends academic weight, moral authority, and theological precision to the conference. More than that, Piper shares Passion's overarching vision. Worship songs from Charlie Hall and Chris Tomlin, preceding talks by Giglio, pound home two themes beloved by Calvinists—God's sovereignty and glory. From there, Giglio encourages students to devote themselves to evangelism and global missions by pointing to the transcendent God of heaven. His appeals go something like this: God is wonderfully, inexpressibly glorious. You are not. But how amazing is it that the very God of the universe invites screwed-up people to give their lives in sold-out service to his eternal kingdom!

Piper attributes the growing attraction of Calvinism to the way Passion pairs demanding obedience with God's grandeur. Even without an explicitly Calvinist appeal, Passion exemplifies how today's Calvinists relate theology to issues of Christian living such as worship, joy, and missions. "They're not going to embrace your theology unless it makes their hearts sing," Piper told me.

This positive, transformational view of theology might be why so many young evangelicals today hum along to TULIP. Even ten years ago, Piper's ensemble boasted far fewer singers. You don't need me to tell you that Calvinism has a bad reputation. If you consider yourself an Arminian, the rival to Calvinism that emphasizes free will over God's sovereignty in salvation, you bristle at teachings such as limited atonement and irresistible grace. With the feel of a beleaguered minority, even proponents sometimes apologize for Calvinism.

"Calvinists have certainly not stood out in the Christian community as especially pure people when it comes to the way they behave,"

Richard Mouw, president of Fuller Theological Seminary in Pasadena, California, writes in *Calvinism in the Las Vegas Airport*. "They have frequently been intolerant, sometimes to the point of taking abusive and violent action toward people with whom they have disagreed. They have often promoted racist policies. And the fact that they have often defended these things by appealing directly to Calvinist teachings suggests that at least something in these patterns may be due to some weaknesses in the Calvinist perspective itself."[6]

Other than endorsing racism and murder, Calvinism is great, Mouw seems to say. And this comes from someone who considers himself a Calvinist. Mouw writes, "While I sincerely subscribe to the TULIP doctrines, I have to admit that, when stated bluntly, they have a harsh feel about them."[7]

Harsh is how most Christians—indeed, most evangelicals—probably feel about the Puritans, among history's most accomplished Calvinists. Oliver Cromwell exemplifies the Puritan cause in Britain. He ruled the isles from 1649 to 1658 after Puritans and their allies beheaded King Charles I. Textbook writers gloss over Cromwell's contemporaries, including spiritual giants John Owen and Richard Baxter. In America, far more recall the 1692 witch trials in Salem, Massachusetts, than later Calvinists who led explosive revivals (George Whitefield) or achieved theological genius (Jonathan Edwards, best known for his sermon "Sinners in the Hands of an Angry God").

Already by the early 1800s during the Second Great Awakening, Calvinism had sustained some serious blows. Infighting plagued the successors to Edwards in New England. Many Southern Presbyterians defended slavery using Scripture. Renowned evangelist Charles Finney, meanwhile, claimed the Reformed heritage but turned many of its teachings upside down.

More recently, Calvinism lost favor as the church growth and charismatic movements swept through American evangelicalism. Church growth principles urged a focus on common-denominator Christian basics, not including doctrines such as predestination. Fast-growing Pentecostal and charismatic churches trace their roots to

---

[6]Richard J. Mouw, *Calvinism in the Las Vegas Airport* (Grand Rapids, MI: Zondervan, 2004), 114–115.
[7]Ibid., 14.

the Wesleyan/holiness tree. To be sure, Calvinism never went away. But it did remain largely quarantined among the ethnic Dutch in the Christian Reformed Church or the Princeton Presbyterians who built Westminster Theological Seminary in Philadelphia.

When I first wrote for *Christianity Today* in September 2006 about the resurgence of Calvinism among young evangelicals,[8] I heard from many pastors, theologians, and lay leaders in these traditional communities. "Um, hello!" they gently reminded me. "What about us? Don't call it a comeback, Hansen. We didn't go anywhere!" Duly noted. Yet for a tradition that claims John Calvin and Martin Luther, Reformed theology had shriveled into a gaunt caricature of its former self. Who but the gallant few at Banner of Truth kept Puritan writings in print? Who but theologians J. I. Packer and R. C. Sproul convened audiences interested in Reformed theology? Who but the small circle of founders-friendly churches recalled that Calvinists founded the Southern Baptist Convention?

Even these stalwarts likely never envisioned that today Sovereign Grace churches pair charismatic worship with Calvinist theology. They still don't know what to make of the radical church planters who fly the Reformed banner as they employ missional evangelism techniques. They probably never expected a pastor with such definite, controversial views to be warmly received by more than twenty thousand college students who dig modern praise music. These are a few of the leads I pursued to learn about the reasons for the latest Calvinist comeback.

After Joshua Harris attended Passion in 1999, he sought Giglio's help to plan a similar event, from which blossomed the current version of his New Attitude conferences. Harris, the thirty-three-year-old senior pastor of Covenant Life Church in Gaithersburg, Maryland, is widely known for his best-selling book *I Kissed Dating Goodbye*. But dating polemics take a backseat these days to leading a thriving church at the heart of the growing Sovereign Grace church network. The compassionate, soft-spoken Harris told me he found Giglio's God-centered focus at Passion to be refreshing. "What I grew up with was so man-centered," Harris said. "It was all about you and what you do and what

---

[8]Collin Hansen, "Young, Restless, Reformed," *Christianity Today*, September 2006, 32; http://www.christianitytoday.com/ct/2006/september/42.32.html.

you accomplish. Even the songs we sang were so self-centered about God: 'Do this for me.'"

It's pretty common to hear Reformed leaders lament modern praise music. They bemoan forgotten hymns, shallow theology, and repetitive refrains. But you won't hear Piper complain—at least not about the good stuff. "The worship songs that are being written and sung today are about a great God," he said. "They have set the stage for the theology. I still don't understand why many churches don't follow that with preaching that gets the theology of the songs. But at least for the Passion movement, that music is very God-exalting. The things that nineteen-year-olds are willing to say about God in their songs is mind-boggling."

Piper could be thinking about a number of songs belted out by the throngs that packed Atlanta's Phillips Arena, normally home to professional basketball and hockey franchises. I considered Chris Tomlin's "Indescribable": "All powerful, untamable, awestruck we fall to our knees as we humbly proclaim you are amazing God." I also recalled one of my favorite songs, "Wholly Yours" by the David Crowder Band: "I am full of earth, you are heaven's worth; I am stained with dirt, prone to depravity; you are everything that is bright and clean, the antonym of me, you are divinity."

These songs from Passion artists illustrate the conference's picture of a transcendent God, untamable and wholly unlike us. With intimate knowledge of our depravity, we respond by falling to our knees—actually at Passion students are more likely to raise and wave their arms. Those physical acts of worship alone prove that these students don't act like Baptists from previous generations. As I watched Passion, I couldn't help but wonder, don't many of these students attend churches where pastors sound a lot like therapists and teach that God just wants us to do good and feel good about ourselves? Some even attend churches that promise health and wealth for faithful believers. If so, why do these youths sing songs about depravity?

Maybe you can only survive so long on a self-help diet. Eventually you get pretty sick of yourself. A biblical understanding of God—big beyond description, active, perfectly holy—tastes much better than junk-food pop psychology. Imagine that this transcendent God still condescended to save his disobedient people. Because he so loved the world, this God of the universe dressed in flesh and suffered on the cross. Yet he did not stay in that tomb. The power of God raised Jesus Christ, who made a way for us to dwell in the house of the Lord forever if we only believe. Transcendent, yet immanent, he transforms us, and then he employs us in transforming the world to renew his creation. For students at Passion, the biblical picture of God feels new, appealing, and exciting.

"I do wonder if some of the appeal [of Calvinism] and the trend isn't a reaction to the watered-down vision of God that's been portrayed in the evangelical seeker-oriented churches," Joshua Harris told me. "I'm not trying to knock them, but I just think that there's such a hunger for the transcendent and for a God who is not just sitting around waiting for us to show up so that the party can get started."

Many churches geared toward so-called spiritual seekers focus on God's immanence, his nearness. They talk about a personal relationship with Christ, emphasizing his friendship and reminding audiences that God made us in his image. It all makes sense, because so many baby boomers left churches that felt impersonal and irrelevant. But the culture has shifted. Fewer Americans now claim any church background. Evangelical megachurches, once the upstart challengers, have become the new mainstream. Teenagers who grew up with buddy Jesus in youth group don't know as much about Father God.

"We live in a transcendence-starved culture and a transcendence-starved evangelicalism," said Timothy George, founding dean of Beeson Divinity School in Birmingham, Alabama. "We've so dumbed down the gospel and dumbed down worship in a good effort to reach as many people as we can that there's almost a backlash. It comes from this great hunger for a genuinely God-centered, transcendence-focused understanding of who God is and what God wants us to do and what God has given us in Jesus Christ. All of that resonates deeply with a kind of pastoral Reformed position that Piper articulates so well."

Indeed, Calvinism puts much stock in transcendence, which draws out biblical themes such as God's holiness, glory, and majesty. Think of the prophet Isaiah's vision in Isaiah 6:1: "In the year that King Uzziah died I saw the Lord sitting upon a throne, high and lifted up; and the train of his robe filled the temple." In Piper's preaching and Passion's music, beholding God's transcendence helps us experience his immanence or nearness. This powerful combination at conferences like Passion blows apart stereotypes of Reformed theology as cold and detached study of God.

"Someone like Louie Giglio is saying, 'You know what, it's not about us, it's about God's glory, it's about his renown,'" Harris said. "Now I don't think most kids realize this, but that's the first step down a pathway of Reformed theology. Because if you say that it's not about you, well, then you're on that road of saying it's not about your actions, your choosings, your determination.

"If you believe that ultimately it is your action, your choosing, your decision—that ultimately your salvation finally gets back to you—that's going to turn into a very moralistic kind of religion," Harris said. "That's why a lot of people I hear from who discover Reformed theology talk about it almost like they got saved for the first time."

A note of caution is in order. If we are to believe history's most thorough study of teenagers' religious attitudes, moralism is still winning. Christian Smith and Melinda Lundquist Denton, the sociologists who conducted that survey, argue that a new religion has supplanted Christianity in America. This religion teaches that "God is something like a combination Divine Butler and Cosmic Therapist: he is always on call, takes care of any problems that arise, professionally helps his people to feel better about themselves, and does not become too personally involved in the process," Smith and Denton argue in *Soul Searching: The Religious and Spiritual Lives of American Teenagers*.[9] They call this religion Moralistic Therapeutic Deism.

Smith and Denton, sociologists with the National Study of Youth and Religion, offer a grim diagnosis. "It is not so much that U.S. Christianity is being secularized," they write. "Rather more subtly, Christianity is either degenerating into a pathetic version of itself or, more significantly, Christianity is actively being colonized and displaced by a quite different religious faith."[10]

Oddly enough, Smith and Denton found that most teenagers like church and appreciate their parents. But hundreds of phone surveys

---

[9]Christian Smith with Melinda Lundquist Denton, *Soul Searching: The Religious and Spiritual Lives of American Teenagers* (New York: Oxford University Press USA, 2005), 165.
[10]Ibid., 171.

and more than two hundred and fifty face-to-face interviews revealed that astonishingly few teenagers can articulate even the basics about their religious beliefs. The students aren't dumb. According to Smith and Denton, they speak intelligently about drug abuse and sexually transmitted diseases, for example. Catechesis isn't dead after all. It's just that many churches and families have ceded this responsibility to public schools. As a result, teenagers can express a deep understanding of toleration but not of justification. They know the problems of teenage pregnancy but do not fear the God who commands holiness.

The raw statistics make you wonder what's going on in evangelical youth groups. Around one-third of the surveyed conservative Protestant teenagers affirmed belief in fortune-tellers, reincarnation, and astrology.[11] More said many religions may be true (48 percent) than affirmed the exclusive truth of one religion (46 percent). Teenagers may like church, but they don't think it's important—64 percent of conservative Protestants responded that believers need not be involved in a religious congregation in order to be truly religious or spiritual.[12]

"What legitimates the religion of most youth today is not that it is the life-transformative, transcendent truth, but that it instrumentally provides mental, psychological, emotional, and social benefits that teens find useful and valuable," Smith and Denton write.[13] They note that almost none of the teenagers talked about God's sovereignty.

If my investigation would find a resurgence of Calvinism, then something must happen to these students after high school. Smith and Denton offer some clues. They found that teenagers have the desire but not the opportunities to learn from adult role models. Rather unrebellious, these teenagers will respond to challenging guidance from caring adults—the kind of messages delivered by John Piper at Passion, for example. Piper struck a nerve in 2000 when he challenged his largest audience—about forty thousand students gathered outside Memphis, Tennessee, on a blustery May day—not to waste their lives pursuing the American dream. The resulting book, *Don't Waste Your Life*, has sold more than 250,000 copies.

Smith and Denton write, "We suspect that there are opportunities

---

[11]Ibid., 44.
[12]Ibid., 74.
[13]Ibid., 154.

to show youth how very conventional they are actually acting, how unexciting they are in their approach to faith, to create discomforts to motivate them to more seriously engage what faith is and might be in their lives."[14]

They warn middle-aged religious leaders not to expect today's youth to think and behave as they did in the more tumultuous 1960s and 1970s. "[O]ur findings suggest to us that religious communities should also stop—again, as we not infrequently observe—presuming that U.S. teenagers are actively alienated by religion, are dropping out of their religious congregations in large numbers, cannot relate to adults in their congregations, and so need some radically new 'postmodern' type of program or ministry."[15]

So what do they need? Though it may be dominant among today's American teenagers, Moralistic Therapeutic Deism cannot save. As evangelicals graduate from high school and leave the churches of their youth, many end up at conferences like Passion or New Attitude and begin to be transformed by the transcendent God they behold through Reformed theology. I suspect that Calvinism strikes a chord with these college-age students precisely because Moralistic Therapeutic Deism has infiltrated so many evangelical youth groups.

In offering this hypothesis, I speak with some experience. I had been a Christian for about two and a half years when I arrived in Evanston, Illinois, in 1999 to study journalism at Northwestern University. During my last two years in high school I had helped lead United Methodist Youth Fellowship at my family's small church in rural South Dakota. The denomination even paid for me to fly to Los Angeles to attend a conference for youth considering full-time ministry.

All the while, my knowledge of Scripture grew little. Sin plagued me with guilt, and I saw little victory over temptation. I'm glad neither Smith nor Denton called to ask me what Christians believe. Yet I knew without a doubt that I had been saved. I recalled with joy the moment my resistance fell and I trusted in Christ to forgive me of my sins. I knew God gave his church the Bible so that we might know about Jesus

---

[14]Ibid., 268.
[15]Ibid., 266.

and learn the story of salvation. I actively shared with unbelieving friends and family about the joy God had given me.

Even before I enrolled, I confirmed that Campus Crusade for Christ ran a chapter at Northwestern. I harbored no false expectations about the climate for Christians at this school that long ago ditched its Methodist roots. I hoped Crusade would help me grow in the faith and introduce me to other students trying to follow Christ. Crusade did that—and much, much more. Our campus director studied for his Master of Divinity degree up the road at Trinity Evangelical Divinity School. Most Crusade students attended a nearby Evangelical Free church, pastored by a Trinity grad. My first morning in church, the pastor rocked my Methodist sensibilities. It wasn't so much the sermon's content that shocked me. Rather, I was surprised the sermon contained any content at all. On top of that, the pastor even raised his voice a few times and preached for more than thirty minutes. That kind of behavior gets you fired by Midwestern Methodists.

I had never heard of Calvinism until a Crusade friend, also a Methodist, told me she believed that God predestines salvation. Before long that's what I believed too. My weekly Bible study with fellow freshmen worked through Romans. An older student took me to hear R. C. Sproul preach. I didn't go looking for Reformed theology. But Reformed theology found me. Beginning college as I did with an almost blank slate, Calvinists impressed me with their knowledge of Scripture and devotion to theological depth. Calvinism made the best sense of what Scripture teaches about salvation. None of this theology seemed to dampen my friends' passion to evangelize the campus and consider serving as missionaries after graduation. As I began teaching Bible studies and mentoring younger students, we discussed Calvinism.

One day between classes I sat eating in a dorm with one of my friends and his academic adviser, a history professor. We began talking about the Puritans and Calvinism—surely the only time this has happened to him before then or since. I professed, "I am a Calvinist."

"Wow!" the professor exclaimed. "I didn't know any of them were still alive."

He proceeded to argue away my Calvinism. He asked how I could reconcile God's sovereignty with free will. He prodded me to see if I thought

God orchestrated the Fall in the Garden of Eden. It wasn't a fair fight. I couldn't match this professor who teaches about intellectual history.

"I'm sorry, but I don't have answers for any of your questions," I responded sheepishly. "I merely believe Calvinism comes closest to honoring the teachings of Jesus and the apostle Paul."

"Oh, if that's your criteria," the professor said, "then you're right."

Believe it or not, that's not the only time Calvinism came up with a professor. During my senior year Northwestern hired a visiting professor to teach about American evangelicalism. More than a hundred and fifty students filled the classroom. About half considered themselves evangelicals and participated in the activities of Crusade or InterVarsity Christian Fellowship, among other groups. During the course's first lecture, the professor, an evangelical himself, surveyed American religious history. Calvinists dominated the First Great Awakening, concentrated in New England, he explained. But their rather frightening view of God dissipated a few decades later during the Second Great Awakening.

"Now only a few Calvinists remain—mostly a few crazies in Grand Rapids," the professor said to classroom laughter.

Taken aback, I approached the professor during the class break. I told him I could point out a number of Calvinists in the room that very day. And I explained that a growing number of Calvinists studied at Trinity, a seminary he had attended decades earlier. What did he make of my pleas? Nothing, really. I was just a student whose name he would never remember. The nation's best universities pay him to teach about evangelical history, culture, and politics.

What I found while investigating youth trends and Calvinism may shock my college professors. It may even surprise a number of evangelicals who don't see the appeal of this difficult theology with a bad reputation. Based on conversations about my previous writing, I know this book will surprise many young Calvinists themselves. As I experienced with our small movement at Northwestern, few have ever viewed these trends from a wider scope. Many who heard Piper speak at Passion and bought *Desiring God* probably never realized they are traveling down a path trod by many of their peers. But they may recognize themselves in these stories of conversion—born again by the power of God, then transformed by the mystery of grace.

CHAPTER TWO

Out of Bethlehem

BETHLEHEM BAPTIST CHURCH
MINNEAPOLIS, MINNESOTA

February isn't the best time to visit Minneapolis. But I couldn't complain, since for months I had persistently lobbied for an interview with John Piper. Now I had an appointment, his last available time before undergoing surgery for prostate cancer and leaving on a five-month sabbatical. Bethlehem Baptist Church offered the sabbatical to their pastor upon serving them for twenty-five years.

The weather didn't let me down. It was just as cold as I thought it would be. In the dead of winter downtown Minneapolis seemed in hibernation. Pulling up to the church, I couldn't believe how close it was to the Metrodome. For years my family watched Twins baseball games nearby, unaware of the thriving if outwardly nondescript church around the corner. Later I learned Piper frequently employs the Metrodome as sermon fodder. Imagine how Puritan preachers chastised their congregations for itching to visit the theater after church and you'll understand Piper when the Vikings play on Sunday afternoon.

Bethlehem is neither fashionable like Rick Warren's Saddleback Church in Orange County, California, nor sprawling like Bill Hybels's Willow Creek Community Church in west suburban Chicago. Bethlehem lacks that most characteristic megachurch feature—ample parking. Good thing I showed up early.

The Saturday evening service felt surprisingly casual. Then again, Minnesota's Scandinavian culture eschews formality and downplays controversy—two reasons I've always been surprised that an intense, controversial pastor like Piper settled here. Still, there was no mistaking

Piper's stamp on the worship service. The congregation sang "I Am on the Battlefield for My Lord," a black gospel hymn that reflected both Piper's commitment to racial harmony and his theological mentality. After the singing, he invited a member of the congregation to stand and recite the week's "fighter verse."

With cancer and sabbatical on his mind, Piper struck a personal note in his sermon. He consciously avoids premeditated humor, but he couldn't help but draw a few laughs from the congregation that evening. "I want you to know it would be my delight to serve you until I'm seventy years old," he said. Decades in Minnesota have failed to eradicate his southern accent. "I've said to the elders many times, 'Look, as soon as I start saying unintelligible, stupid, embarrassing things, would you just mercifully and quickly call me emeritus?'" The audience's relaxed chuckles indicated obvious affection for their longtime pastor.

Piper's sermon, based on 1 Corinthians 1:10–31, aimed to make sure that affection for him didn't hold up the church while he stole away for the summer. Unlike some popular preachers who deliver generic Bible messages, you could tell Piper had prepared his sermon with certain church members in mind. He called out a couple of elders—not by name—who said the church goes into a holding pattern when Pastor John is gone.

Piper hit his stride as he cast a vision for his church. It would be an understatement to describe Piper as animated in the pulpit. His gestures match his theology. Piper lifts the gaze of his audience toward a mighty, transcendent God. "Would it not be just like God to choose a time when the big-shot preacher is away to bring the greatest awakening— the greatest ingathering of souls, the greatest giving, the greatest sending, the greatest season of signs and wonders, the greatest worship, the greatest impact on the world?"

The passage's repeated descriptions of God calling and choosing did not escape Piper. If his calling card is God's glory, Piper has also become known as an ardent advocate of Calvinism. His sermon fused these two interests. "That's how all of you got saved who are saved," he said. "And you will give God a lot more glory if you know it and embrace it and praise him for it. The cross became irresistibly beautiful. You could not but freely embrace it."

At sixty years old, Piper is the chief spokesman for the Calvinist resurgence among young evangelicals. Ten years of Passion conferences have introduced him to a generation of young evangelicals. More than three thousand pastors heard Piper deliver a keynote address in 2006 at Together for the Gospel, which also featured R. C. Sproul and John MacArthur. The conference organizers—Mark Dever, Ligon Duncan, C. J. Mahaney, and Al Mohler—seemed ever conscious of the stoic man seated directly in front of them in the first row, watching over them for three days like a grandfather observing his son with grandchildren. Nearly every story I heard while traveling included lessons learned from at least one of Piper's many best-selling books, especially *Desiring God*.

"John has the gift of catching the attention of young thinking people and getting them excited about thinking as an exercise, because he himself does it so passionately," theologian J. I. Packer told me. "He gives them the sense that passionate thinking is at the essence of real life."

I visited Piper in Minneapolis to find out how he has caught the attention of young evangelicals. What's so captivating about his passion for God's glory? What is bringing Calvinism back in style? I also wanted to meet the youth who sit under his preaching every week. What's so appealing about a pastor who cites Jonathan Edwards, a long-dead Calvinist who got fired from his church? Do they really buy into total depravity and unconditional election? Finally, I planned to explore a common critique of Piper, that so-called Piperites pledge him unhealthy allegiance. I traveled to Minneapolis because you can't study Calvinism without dropping by Geneva.

After the evening service, Matt Van Zee stuck around to answer some of my questions. Casual dress and an earring might have branded Matt with the emerging church. Arms raised during worship might have pegged him charismatic. He quickly assured me that despite the last name, he knew nothing about the Dutch Reformed tradition. Matt said he first learned about Calvinism while attending a Christian high school in the Twin Cities area.

"When we first learned what Calvinism is, it struck everybody like, 'Whoa, God predestined? That's really terrible.'" I'd guess most Calvinists have either shared this thought at one point or at least heard others react that way. Matt started reading the New Testament for himself as a junior in high school. Ephesians 1 and Romans 9 stuck out. "Calvin wasn't just being difficult," Matt said. "He was seeking to systematize what I was seeing in Scripture."

Matt didn't consider his story to be unique. "People are brought up with one conception of Calvinism as the stale 'frozen chosen,'" he explained. "Or they're like me and haven't previously read the Scriptures themselves, so when they do they're like, 'Whoa, wait a second. There is a pretty strong theme throughout the Old and New Testament of God's extreme sovereignty over the wills and decisions of people.'"

Matt's pastor would be pleased with how the twenty-five-year-old described Calvinism to me. Mere knowledge is not the end of Calvinism or any other theology. Theology should drive a Christian toward transformation—toward greater worship of God and more powerful service for his sake.

"Calvinism is such a comfort and a means to follow Christ more passionately," Matt said. "I feel pretty overwhelmed by my sin a lot of the time. And when I evangelize, I reach this point with people where I can't convince them. I've studied; I've tried my best. And what do I pray for? *God, break their heart. Make the cross irresistibly compelling so they just see there's no other hope.*"

I could already tell Matt didn't fit the buttoned-down bookworm stereotype of Calvinists. Despite strong convictions, he didn't seem eager to wield his theology as a sword. When studying at Bethel University, Matt steered clear of the late-night dorm debates when fellow students clashed over grace and free will. "I just want people to have a biblical position," he said. "If they've searched Scripture and honestly come to the conclusion that Arminianism is the truth, good."

Still, Matt couldn't help but wonder how many evangelicals deny God's sovereign purposes for the same reason he did at first—because he didn't want to concede that much control to God. He sure doesn't have that problem now. Like other young Calvinists I interviewed, Matt has made his peace with hard doctrines. A Charles Spurgeon quote comes to mind: "I know of no such thing as paring off the rough edges of a doctrine."[1] Non-Calvinists have longed chafed at this sort of response, which they say alienates unbelievers. Calvinists, in turn, argue that some Christians have compromised biblical fidelity for apologetic appeasement.

"It seems like there is this urge to defend God for things he doesn't even defend himself against," Matt explained. "There's a search to let God off the hook for problems in the world as if he's not in control of them, when in the Bible there are passages like, 'Does disaster come to a city, unless the LORD has done it?' [Amos 3:6] And in Lamentations 3, 'Is it not from the mouth of the Most High that good and bad come?' [v. 38]. That was an answer to something that long troubled me about God's sovereignty. Even today I'm struggling with an ongoing sequence of frustrations in some relationships. To believe that God is sovereign is very comforting in the deepest way possible."

I wrapped up talking with Matt around the same time Piper finished greeting and praying for people following the service. After we headed back out into the cold, Piper surprised me by hopping in my rented Jeep and directing me the few blocks to his house. I can think of many pastors who wouldn't rely on a stranger to give them a ride home. As we began talking in the car, I was still thinking about that morning, when Piper called me as I rode to O'Hare Airport in Chicago to catch the flight to Minneapolis. We talked briefly to plan our meeting, and he told me that he sits down for a bowl of cereal after delivering his Saturday night sermon. That seemed convenient—I mentioned that I would need to eat as well. I inadvertently invited myself over for dinner. Piper said his wife, Noël, would make us something.

After only a couple of minutes we arrived at Piper's modest home, decorated with an inviting, midwestern flavor. He snuck away to tuck his young daughter, Talitha, into bed, leaving me alone to collect my thoughts for the interview. I quickly understood another reason why Piper looked forward to the five-month sabbatical studying at Tyndale House in Cambridge, England. Inside the house, even on a Saturday night, you can hear the steady drone of traffic on nearby Interstate 94.

I looked around and did not see a television, recalling what Piper

---

[1]Quoted in Iain Murray, *The Forgotten Spurgeon* (Edinburgh: Banner of Truth, 1972), 55–56.

wrote in *Don't Waste Your Life*. "Television is one of the greatest time-wasters of the modern age. . . . The greatest problem is banality. A mind fed daily on TV diminishes. Your mind was made to know and love God. Its facility for this great calling is ruined by excessive TV."[2]

Piper had just returned and started our conversation when Noël told us she had finished preparing dinner. As we settled down with our soup, Piper said he had not considered a generational dimension to the resurgence of Reformed theology. But he had noticed with pleasure a general revival of the doctrines of grace, those beliefs held dear by Calvinism. A sure sign of the resurgence is the resulting conflict.

"One of the most common things I deal with when talking to younger pastors is conflict with their senior pastors," Piper explained. "They're youth pastors and they've gone to Trinity Evangelical Divinity School and read something R. C. Sproul or I wrote and they say, 'We're really out of step. What should we do?' I try to say you have to be totally candid with your pastor and tell him where you're coming from and pray that God will help him share your vision. And then ask permission. And if they give you permission, teach away. Build your movement."

Piper himself has built a remarkable following. His signature book, *Desiring God*, has sold more than 275,000 copies. It's practically required reading for many college-age evangelicals, though he didn't write it especially for youth. Still, his energy and passion click with youth who embrace his calls to radical joy and obedience delivered at conferences such as Resolved in Southern California or New Attitude in Louisville, Kentucky. His relentlessly serious demeanor does not so much intimidate as challenge. He challenges what you believe, how you spend your time, what you really worship.

"John is truly an evangelist, an apologist, a biblical expositor who is almost synonymous with the word *passion*," said Timothy George, dean of Beeson Divinity School. "John connects with the upcoming yuppie generation to make Reformed theology not only palatable but desirable as a way of honoring God with great passion."

Piper has personally taken his message of "Christian hedonism" around the world to diverse venues. Audiences perk up when they hear

---

[2]John Piper, *Don't Waste Your Life* (Wheaton, IL: Crossway Books, 2003), 120.

him tweak the famous opening line from the Westminster Confession: "The chief end of man is to glorify God *by* enjoying him forever."[3] His Desiring God ministry, launched in 1994 after being approved by Bethlehem Baptist Church's elders, sponsors themed national and regional conferences and a yearly event for pastors. Desiring God started because demand grew for his sermons. But the ministry's decision to make all his messages available for free download has expanded demand all the more. Listeners need not even register. Nothing but time hindered Robin Treto from listening to two hundred sermons. By discounting books and often allowing customers to pay whatever they can afford, Desiring God signals that Piper cares most about the message. Because Piper directs all book proceeds back to the ministry and his church, Desiring God reaches wider audiences.

Some animated preachers step down from the pulpit and carry their extroverted personality into board meetings, meet-and-greet events, and one-on-one interviews. You know with many Christian leaders that they would make excellent salesmen, politicians, or fraternity presidents. That's not to be critical. I'm just observing that God endows some with special charisma, which he appropriates for kingdom purposes. Piper does not fit this description. While maintaining full seriousness with me, he shifted from boisterous to meek. He listened actively and intently as I explained my project. This behind-the-scenes Piper more closely matches his physical traits. You would have to be looking for Piper to notice him in a crowd. Who notices the scrawny grandfather with tufts of thinning, wavy hair on a mostly bald head?

And that's the way I think he would want it. Piper does not want anything to distract from his message. Piper's eloquence wins hearers. But you've missed his point if you hear him speak and walk away marveling at anything but the source of his renowned passion.

"My whole project theologically is to say that God is more God-centered than any other being in the universe, and then to back that up with dozens of texts that say God does everything for his glory," Piper explained to me. "God is most glorified when we're most satisfied in him. Affections are central—not just marginal—and it's okay to be happy in God."

---

[3]John Piper, *Desiring God* (Sisters, OR: Multnomah, 1996), 15.

More than the five points of Calvinism, this is what Piper wants you to understand. But without Piper's infusion of God-given zeal, I doubt Calvinism would have recaptured the affection of young evangelicals. Piper knows how opponents have caricatured Calvinists, sometimes with merit. Like his hero, Jonathan Edwards, Piper invigorates Calvinism with a passion for piety.

"I think the criticism of Reformed theology is being silenced by the mission and justice and evangelism and worship and counseling—the whole range of pastoral life," Piper said. "We're not the kind who are off in a Grand Rapids ghetto crossing our t's and dotting our i's and telling the world to get their act together. We're in the New Orleans slums with groups like Desire Street Ministries, raising up black elders through Reformed theology from nine-year-old boys who had no chance."

The next morning I returned to Bethlehem for Sunday worship. During the first service I wandered around the church, including the bookstore. As you might expect, the bookstore speaks volumes about Piper and his church. For that matter, the bookstore characterizes the entire Calvinist resurgence. Piper's contributions alone take up almost one entire wall, illustrating his prolific reach. While writing and contributing to nearly thirty-five books, Piper doesn't use ghostwriters, an increasingly common practice among popular evangelical authors. I found the shelves stocked with anything but your typical Christian bookstore fare. Volumes for sale included theological classics such as Martin Luther's *Bondage of the Will*, John Calvin's *Institutes of the Christian Religion*, John Owen's *Of the Mortification of Sin in Believers*, and Jonathan Edwards's *Freedom of the Will*. Equally telling were the Christian best-sellers I didn't see.

Seven portraits encircle the bookshelves—Augustine, Luther, Calvin, Owen, Bunyan, Edwards, Spurgeon. The first three speak to the movement's proudly Reformational orientation. Martin Luther affirmed Augustine of Hippo's theology of original sin and predestination. Luther also pioneered the Protestant view of justification, a vitally important belief then and now. Piper has spent good chunks of recent years writing detailed scholarly defenses of the traditional Protestant understanding of justification.[4] The third portrait, that of John Calvin, commemorates the profound theological system he bequeathed to Protestants.

The other four portraits explain even more. In many ways the Calvinist resurgence Piper is leading owes more to the British Puritans than even Calvin or any other stream of Reformed theology. John Owen, known for penetrating insight into sanctification, emerged as the top theologian from the era of Puritan rule in Britain. John Bunyan endured persecution for his Puritan faith and produced the defining work of Christian pilgrimage literature, *Pilgrim's Progress*. Charles Spurgeon, a Baptist like Bunyan, zealously evangelized and during the 1800s built possibly the world's first megachurch. Jonathan Edwards, the only American whose portrait hung in the library, died nearly two decades before the colonies became the United States. In recommending *Desiring God*, J. I. Packer said, "Jonathan Edwards, whose ghost walks through most of Piper's pages, would be delighted with his disciple."

As much as I enjoyed the bookstore, I was just killing time while awaiting the morning's big event. I couldn't believe my good fortune. It just so happened the college group was learning the five points of Calvinism, TULIP. You can safely bet Piper's vision has thoroughly penetrated the church if the college students are studying TULIP.

There's something about high-school and college groups that still makes me uncomfortable. They take me back to awkward days as the new kid in high-school youth group or a freshman in Campus Crusade. Of course, I had nothing to fear—this group seemed friendly enough. The students converged on Bethlehem from colleges all over the Twin Cities, especially Bethel and the University of Minnesota. Following a few worship songs accompanied by guitar, a recent graduate serving with Campus Outreach stood up to deliver the morning's lecture. With the tinge of a southern accent that probably helps keep his dance card full, he began addressing the topic of unconditional election.

"If you really believe Ephesians 2:1, that you are dead in your trespasses and sins, then you are spiritually incapacitated. You are spiritually incapable. You are floating bloated," Andrew Knight told the

---

[4]See John Piper, *Counted Righteous in Christ: Should We Abandon the Imputation of Christ's Righteousness?* (Wheaton, IL: Crossway Books, 2002) and John Piper, *The Future of Justification: A Response to N. T. Wright* (Wheaton, IL: Crossway Books, 2007).

group. "You don't just need a little help in your present situation. You are in need of a rescue." Logically, last week's subject must have been total depravity. Andrew continued to diagnose the spiritual state of humanity. He delivered a powerful Augustinian case for original sin.

"We have a plague of immorality. It's not that you really desire to do good and you have the best of intentions, but you just can't carry it out. Your aspirations, your motivation, the inclinations of your heart—like Genesis 6:5 and Genesis 8:21 say—the thoughts of the heart are only evil continually. Paul says in Romans 7:18, 'There is nothing good that dwells in me.' Isaiah 64:6 reinforces this—even my most righteous acts, the best I have to offer on his altar—these are insufficient. Finally, in Romans 3, Paul again emphasizes that there is no one who's righteous. No, not one. There's not one who seeks God. All have turned away. Remind yourself that justice says we deserve hell. You are so bad that you deserve an eternity away from the God of the world."

That's a pretty serious departure from the self-esteem pep talks these students must have heard from teachers growing up. Calvinists don't think much of self-esteem. It seems every Puritan claimed to be the chief of sinners. But how bad could John Bunyan have been, really? Two shillings say my sins could top that ole tinker. See, there I go. It's infectious.

Emphasizing total depravity, the *t* in TULIP does draw out a couple of important points. First, it deflects glory to a truly wonderful and mysterious God who would elect even me, the worst person I know. Second, it underscores how election is unconditional, the *u* in TULIP. Surely God found nothing worthy in me to make him want to grant me the inheritance of eternal bliss.

"Our morality is not enough," Andrew continued. "So what do we have to hope in for our salvation, for our rescue? The adjective in front of the word *election* has to read *unconditional* because if it's conditional, then we're damned. That's why Paul spent so much time in Ephesians reminding us how we were saved, because we did nothing to inherit our position before God. There's nothing you will ever do, there's nothing you have done that will ever earn God's salvation, his election, his rescue."

Andrew proceeded to work through some common election passages, such as Titus 3:4–5 and Ephesians 1:5. "It's not distant. It's not stoic. It's not a disinterested lottery pick," Andrew said. He illustrated the point by gesturing to individuals scattered throughout the audience. "It's up close and personal, face to face, personal, intimate, unconditional election. You may never feel the weight, you will never feel the wonder of grace until you finally relinquish your claim to have any part in your salvation. It has to be unconditional."

Piper devotes a chapter to election in *The Pleasures of God*. He observes, "It seems there is something about the truth of God's free and sovereign election that stands guard over the mind and heart of the church and keeps her alert to tendencies and shifts that swing wide from the plumb line of God's Word."[5] Piper would not be the first Calvinist to argue that the doctrines of grace help Christians ward off liberalism.

Don't get Roger Olson started on this topic. The Truett Seminary professor in Waco, Texas, taught at Bethel for years and occasionally crossed paths with Piper. "When Piper speaks, he gives you the impression that he absolutely knows truth," Olson told me. "Young students are not used to that." As I began researching this project, I asked a number of sources whom I should reach to discuss the opposition to Calvinism. Olson's name surfaced with every source. I reached Olson by phone and had no trouble orienting him to my topic. Fortunately for me Olson had recently finished his book *Arminian Theology: Myths and Realities*.

Olson began teaching theology at Bethel in 1984. At the time Olson and other faculty members identified a handful of "Piper cubs" or "Piperites," devotees of the Bethlehem pastor who taught at the college from 1974 to 1980. That group increased in number over the next fifteen years.

"When I left Bethel College in 1999 and came to Truett, I thought I'd left John Piper behind," Olson said. "But he was the first person my students asked me about, and after him Jesse Ventura and Garrison Keillor, because I'm from Minnesota." Even in Texas, almost every one of his seminary students has either read a Piper book, visited the Desiring God web site, or heard him speak at a Passion conference.

---

[5]John Piper, *The Pleasures of God: Meditations on God's Delight in Being God* (Sisters, OR: Multnomah, 2000), 145.

"College students will hear him at a place like Passion talk about giving their whole lives to missions and the glory of God," Olson said. "Some of them go further and start reading his books and start reading Sproul, start networking with others, get into the Reformed University Fellowship perhaps.

"Those students, in my experience, begin often to think [Calvinism] is the gospel, and that anyone who doesn't agree with it—like myself—isn't authentically Christian."

Arminianism stands against Calvinism as its theological foil. The system draws its name from the Dutch theologian Jacob Arminius (1560–1609), who challenged the prevailing views of his colleagues. In fact, Calvinists produced the TULIP acronym at the Synod of Dordt in 1618 and 1619 in response to followers of Arminius. Today wide swaths of Protestantism similarly disagree with Calvinism, including Methodists, Wesleyans, Nazarenes, Anabaptists, Pentecostals, and many Lutherans who chose not to follow in Luther's footsteps on God's sovereignty in salvation.

As a general rule of thumb, Arminians believe that God limits himself and affords us broader freedom than Calvinists allow. Olson appropriately defines Calvinism more broadly than just TULIP. "Calvinism is that theology which emphasizes God's absolute sovereignty as the all-determining reality, especially with regard to salvation."[6] This definition cuts to the heart of the matter, particularly on election. Non-Calvinists want no part of a God who could save everyone but chooses not to. They believe God chooses to leave that decision up to us. Otherwise, Arminians argue, a relationship with God would be coerced and thereby not genuine.

"What Arminians deny is not predestination but unconditional predestination," Olson writes. "[T]hey embrace conditional predestination based on God's foreknowledge of who will freely respond positively to God's gracious offer of salvation and the prevenient enablement to accept it."[7]

Early Arminians and some other non-Calvinists today join Calvinists to affirm total depravity—we are helpless in original sin without God's

---

[6]Roger E. Olson, *Arminian Theology: Myths and Realities* (Downers Grove, IL: InterVarsity Press, 2006), 15.
[7]Ibid., 19.

grace. That's the easiest doctrine to empirically prove. Arminians don't seem to tout this doctrine like Calvinists though. According to some Calvinists, that's because the Arminian view of total depravity is diminished by their disagreement with other elements of TULIP.

Common ground is harder to find on limited atonement. Olson explains, "Arminians believe that Christ's death on the Cross provides a universal remedy for the guilt of inherited sin so that it is not imputed to infants for Christ's sake."[8] Even many Calvinists can tick off the other four points before stumbling on limited atonement (also known as particular redemption or definite atonement). Did Jesus die only for the sins of the church, the elect? Does not God make the invitation to faith universal in John 3:16? "For God so loved the world, that he gave his only Son, that whoever believes in him should not perish but have eternal life."

Piper and his church staff answer this and other questions in their helpful document, "What We Believe About the Five Points of Calvinism."[9] They argue that if Christ died for everyone, then the cross did not effectively purchase redemption for anyone in particular. The Bethlehem staff explains, "In order to say that Christ died for all men in the same way, the Arminian must limit the atonement to a powerless opportunity for men to save themselves from their terrible plight of depravity." This does not account for passages like John 10:15 where Jesus seems to have the church in view: "I lay down my life for the sheep." As for the universal invitation, Calvinists do not deny that Jesus' death was sufficient to accomplish salvation for all. But with passages like John 3:16, Calvinists interpret "the world" to parallel the situation in Revelation 5:9: "Worthy are you to take the scroll and to open its seals, for you were slain, and by your blood you ransomed people for God from every tribe and language and people and nation." So "the world," then, refers not to every person but to people from every corner of the globe.

Arminians don't deny the work of God in salvation through grace. But they substitute "prevenient grace" for irresistible grace (or

---

[8]Ibid., 33.
[9]Bethlehem Baptist Church Staff, "What We Believe About the Five Points of Calvinism," Desiring God, http://www.desiringgod.org/ResourceLibrary/Articles/ByDate/1985/1487_What_We_Believe_About_the_Five_Points_of_Calvinism/.

"effectual calling"), the fourth point of TULIP. Prevenient grace affords us free will to accept or reject salvation. God issues this kind of grace through gospel proclamation, for example. Calvinists counter that total depravity renders us unwilling to choose God when given the freedom to accept or reject him. John 6:44 illustrates this process. Jesus explains, "No one can come to me unless the Father who sent me draws him. And I will raise him up on the last day."

Finally, Arminians do not offer a united front on the last point of TULIP—perseverance of the saints. Arminians in the wide-reaching Wesleyan stream, for example, teach that Christians may fall away from God. But some classic Arminians affirm with Calvinists that God sustains believers to endure in the faith to the end. The God who began the salvation process with election will one day bring it to completion (Phil. 1:6). Jesus promises in John 10:28, "I give them eternal life, and they will never perish, and no one will snatch them out of my hand."

If you don't like Calvinism but disavow the Arminian label, you're not alone. Olson writes, "Arminianism is almost totally unknown, let alone believed, in popular evangelical Christianity."[10] Furthermore, Olson explains, "To the best of my knowledge no book currently in print in English is devoted solely to explaining Arminianism as a system of theology."[11]

Many simply call themselves Wesleyan, Pentecostal, or Baptist. But many others—perhaps even most evangelicals, according to Olson— affirm yet another option. "The gospel preached and the doctrine of salvation taught in most evangelical pulpits and lecterns, and believed in most evangelical pews, is not classical Arminianism but semi-Pelagianism if not outright Pelagianism."[12]

So what is Pelagianism? Pelagius (354–420/440) clashed with Augustine over original sin and the effect of grace. R. C. Sproul explains Pelagius's teaching: "Sin is always an act and never a nature. Otherwise, Pelagius insisted, God would be the author of evil."[13] Furthermore,

---

[10]Olson, *Arminian Theology: Myths and Realities*, 31.
[11]Ibid., 12.
[12]Ibid., 30.
[13]R. C. Sproul, *Willing to Believe: The Controversy Over Free Will* (Grand Rapids, MI: Baker Books, 2002), 37.

Pelagius said that since God tells us to believe, we must possess the power to believe without the help of God's grace.

Prevenient grace distinguishes Arminianism from semi-Pelagianism, which teaches that we can initiate our own salvation. Semi-Pelagians still deny that we can complete our salvation—that's left for full-blown Pelagians. Olson traces this problem in American evangelicalism back to nineteenth-century revivalist Charles Finney, who Olson says denied original sin and the need for prevenient grace.[14] Evangelicals today borrow heavily from Finney, a leading figure in the Second Great Awakening.

If Olson is correct, then Calvinists and Arminians can team up against the Pelagians. But Olson wants an apology first from Calvinists who have lumped all non-Calvinists together. "Let's talk. Read my book," Olson told me. "Then let's see what they think now about Arminianism. We're going to find that we agree that semi-Pelagianism is a heresy that is extremely popular—maybe the default heresy of American Christianity and evangelicalism included."

Those are tough words. But they are appropriate words if you think Christians act according to what they believe. This conviction about the practicality of theology is so crucial to Calvinist thinking that few bothered to even remind me that this is why they spend so much time discovering and debating doctrine. "From the very beginning, we are speaking to them God-centered, Christ-exalting truths that shatter fallen human categories of thought," Piper told the Bethlehem Conference for Pastors in 2005. "We must not shy away from this. We must do all we can to advance it and to help people, by the grace of God, to see what is happening to them [the shattering of their categories] as the best news in the world."

Calvinists argue that trials in particular expose what we believe, which dictates how we respond. Charles Spurgeon observed, "When one is full of health and vigor, and has everything going well, you might, perhaps, live on the elementary truths of Christianity very comfortably; but in times of stern pressure of spirit, when the soul is much cast down, you want the marrow and the fatness. In

---

[14]Olson, *Arminian Theology: Myths and Realities*, 27.

times of inward conflict, salvation must be all of grace from first to last."[15]

Following Andrew Knight's talk for the college group, I sat down with two young women who told me about how Calvinism affects the way they practice their faith. Carmela Cirafesi, twenty-six, works with Campus Outreach, a ministry with origins in the Presbyterian Church in America (PCA). As we talked, her concern and care for college women was evident. She spoke of them with the empathetic heart of an evangelist, eager to build friendships and relate to them the good news of Jesus Christ. But apparently she wasn't always this way. Carmela grew up with Calvinism as she attended a PCA church. Looking back, she heard about evangelism a lot more than she saw it. The "frozen chosen" rested easy in the confidence that if God had to join a denomination, he'd be a Presbyterian, Carmela said.

Her whole perspective changed one summer during college at Emory University in Atlanta. She traveled on a mission project with Campus Outreach. "For the first time I saw people who were passionate about God and about people who believed that God had complete control over salvation," Carmela explained. "Someone made a comment to me that summer that has stuck with me ever since—never, ever in the Bible do people initiate a relationship with God."

Laura Watkins also grew up in a Christian family. But her evangelical church boasted no such doctrinal overconfidence. Quite the opposite, actually. "It was more like, 'I love Jesus, we love Jesus, that's good,'" said Watkins, twenty-one. She moved to Minneapolis to attend the University of Minnesota. After overhearing some other students chatting about Bethlehem, Laura showed up during one of her first weeks in the Twin Cities.

"The first Sunday Pastor John kind of scared me a little bit," she remembered. "I was used to a very conversational preaching style. Having someone wave his arms and talk really loudly made me a little scared."

Laura didn't seem to be the type who would be scared off by some demonstrative, passionate preaching. The short brunette related her story to me with abundant energy and confidence. I think every good

---

[15]Quoted in Murray, *The Forgotten Spurgeon*, 83.

youth group has a girl like Laura, whose joy inspires others to shake off complacency and fear. Or maybe Piper's passion has really rubbed off on Laura over four years. But it wasn't Piper who kept her coming back to Bethlehem at first. "I met some people that first Sunday and just saw a level of spiritual maturity in the church that attracted me, because at that time of my life I wanted to grow spiritually, I just wasn't sure how," she told me. "That's what kept me coming back."

Calvinism wasn't a draw either. "The only exposure I had was high-school textbooks that teach about John Calvin as this crazy guy who burned people," Laura said. "I had this bad feeling. When people mentioned Calvinism I was like, 'Oh my goodness, like, they believe that here?'"

I've been there. I reacted the same way at first to Jonathan Edwards, before developing deep respect for him. After my wife and I had been married more than a year, I found out she still thought that way about Edwards, even as I read George Marsden's *Jonathan Edwards: A Life* before going to sleep. I'm still not sure what she thought when she watched me diligently work through a biography of the preacher she only knew from "Sinners in the Hands of an Angry God." That much-anthologized sermon has done much to confuse high schoolers about the Puritan legacy.

Like everyone else I spoke with at Bethlehem, Laura said that simple exposure to Bible passages such as Ephesians 1 and 2 Timothy 1:9 eroded her resistance to Calvinism. Looking back she could see how God had worked through events and other people to bring her to salvation. But conversion to Calvinism didn't just change the way she recalled her salvation. It emboldened her evangelism.

"Lately I've been thinking about how Reformed theology frees me up to do ministry," Laura said. "I have a real passion for missions, and I was over in the Middle East last summer. It was really hard to be there because I was in a town where missionaries have been active for more than a decade, but not a single person has come to faith."

Somehow this disappointment did not discourage Laura. She even rejoiced in God's sovereignty. "It was the most freeing thing to realize that their salvation is not dependent on me spending enough time with them or me explaining the gospel in the best way or me being an expert in the language," she explained. "It freed me up to love being there even if I wasn't seeing fruit."

But really, now, would she not grow discouraged if she prayed and labored for years without anything to show for the effort? "If you don't go into Reformed theology with the idea that you deserve to go to hell, then it's not going to make any sense because you'll wonder how God could be so unfair," she answered. "But then you realize it's unfair that we're being led to heaven in the first place. We start out as enemies of God; so if he chooses not to save us, that's perfectly just."

Carmela and Laura made my job easy. It was apparent that they spent considerable time thinking about these questions before I dropped by their church. I was especially intrigued to hear how they would respond to my next set of questions. The Calvinist resurgence is a complementarian movement. That is, these Calvinists understand from Scripture that men should lead churches and households. I wondered how Carmela and Laura navigated a theology that Piper admitted appeals to masculine instincts. Olson told me he had never known a female student who switched her beliefs to Calvinism.

Neither Carmela nor Laura told me she entered college with plans to graduate as a submissive housewife. And neither struck me as particularly demure. Yet both delivered ringing endorsements for complementarian relationships. They admitted that it's easier to submit when responsible, capable men abound, as is the case at Bethlehem. Complementarian theology "actually frees women to have leadership in the right context," Carmela explained. Laura didn't seem to have much patience for women who chafed at complementarian expectations. "Girls out there who don't want to submit, that's a sin issue they need to work through," she said. "I think that's what Eve was tempted with in the beginning. I've been convicted about that in my own life."

Still, I wondered how Calvinism relates to complementarian theology. There is nothing about unconditional election or irresistible grace that dictates what you think about gender roles. Or so I thought. "This is a different trait in me, but I see how they connect in my head. I believe God is sovereign and has ordered things in a particular way," Laura explained. "Just as he's chosen those who are going to know him before the foundations of the earth, I don't want to be rebelling against the way God ordered men and women to relate to one another. He's a good God, so it will be in my best interest to be submissive in a biblical way."

Even if neither Laura nor Carmela considered Piper a draw when they began attending Bethlehem, they have come to greatly appreciate his leadership and preaching. "I fell in love with Pastor John, and now I feel as though he's my dad," Laura said. "We've never talked, but I feel really close to him because he has had such an impact on my life; so I'm really thankful to God for his ministry."

Piper openly worries that some people feel great affection for him but don't remember to thank God, as Laura does. It's a catch-22. Charismatic personalities draw the largest audiences. Piper wants other Christians to catch his vision for a glorious God. How better to pass along that vision than to show others how these beliefs have flamed your passions? Maybe it's inevitable that some will miss the message in their attraction to the messenger.

George Whitefield might have been the original American idol. Before the American Revolution, the itinerant evangelist gathered crowds as large as his booming voice could reach. Even skeptical Benjamin Franklin marveled at Whitefield's ability to stir the soul and exact his desired response—faith in Jesus Christ. Yet the contemporary of Jonathan Edwards worried that many in the crowds missed the point. "You have my person too much in admiration," Whitefield wrote to a journalist. "If you look to the instrument less and toward God more, it will be better."[16]

Barnabas Piper has had a front-row seat to observe his father's ministry and his many fans. It's hard enough being a normal pastor's kid. Many PKs breathe a sigh of relief when they leave home for college and escape the spotlight. That doesn't happen when your dad is John Piper and you attend his alma mater, Wheaton College.

Barnabas loved growing up with his father. But before graduating from Wheaton in 2004 he never escaped the intrusive interest in John

---

[16]Quoted in Arnold Dallimore, *George Whitefield: The Life and Times of the Great Evangelist of the Eighteenth-Century Revival*, Vol. 1 (Edinburgh: Banner of Truth, 1970), 402.

Piper's son. "I took on novelty status with some of my fellow students," he told me. "With the rising popularity of Reformed theology among young people, my father has become a celebrity. He never sought this status; he simply preached and wrote about those truths he has seen to be most dear and most powerful. He has accepted his status without reveling in it and has remained humble and grounded.

"It seems that many people, however, have begun to worship John Piper and those like him more than they worship the God these men are desperately striving to point people toward. It is a misplaced fixation on the mouthpiece of truth, the by-product of which deadens the message itself."

Worshiping John Piper. What a bitter irony. Piper seems aware of the problem. "The test of whether you are seeing and savoring Christ or humanly drawn to me will now be put to the test," Piper told his congregation when I visited shortly before he left on sabbatical. "My prayer and hope is that you will show in these next five months that your allegiance is not primarily to me."

CHAPTER THREE

Big Man on Campus

YALE UNIVERSITY
NEW HAVEN, CONNECTICUT

I wasn't surprised to see Irene Sun flipping through a Jonathan Edwards reader one day during a class we audited together at Trinity Evangelical Divinity School. Doug Sweeney, our professor for the class on Protestant thought in the nineteenth century, spent a few weeks teaching about the church leaders who followed Edwards, the eighteenth-century theological giant. I asked Irene, twenty-five, if she liked Edwards. Before long I understood that "like" wouldn't cut it with Irene.

As we walked toward the library after class, Irene told me how reading the thoughts and writings of Edwards sustained her during her years at Yale Divinity School. Studying for a master's degree, Irene struggled to cope with the inclusive theology she learned at Yale. She grew up in Malaysia, where biblical authority was not questioned among the persecuted Christian minority. During her time at Yale, Irene found a lifeline in phone dates with her boyfriend, who studied at a small Minnesota seminary. Hundreds of miles apart, they read Edwards's *Religious Affections* to each other over the phone.

Once Irene told me about their phone dates, I had to hear more. I got that chance over dinner with Irene and Hans, the boyfriend who is now her husband. They invited me to join them in their tidy one-bedroom apartment on Trinity's campus. Hans, forty, is pursuing a PhD in systematic theology, while Irene is pursuing a second master's in Old Testament. Once finished at Trinity, Irene and Hans plan to train pastors and missionaries in China. Both trace their family trees to China. Six generations ago, Irene's ancestors were among the first Chinese to embrace the gospel after western missionaries arrived. Irene's parents, like four other generations of her ancestors, serve as pastors.

During her first three years in the United States, Irene studied at a liberal arts college of the Evangelical Lutheran Church in America. But severe culture shock threatened her faith. Irene couldn't understand why her roommate, who didn't believe in God, attended a Lutheran youth group. That same roommate, twenty-two, invited her fifteen-year-old boyfriend to sleep over. Irene assumed this was typical for American Christianity. So for two years she visited numerous churches but found none she felt she could call home. As a result she faltered in her walk with the Lord for the next several years.

After graduating from Wartburg, Irene took a job in Denver teaching at-risk youth. Spiritual renewal came as she connected with a Chinese evangelical church. Rewarded by the teaching experience and invigorated in her faith, Irene made plans to attend seminary. She ran some possible schools past a new friend. That friend was Hans, who taught Sunday school at a Minnesota church that her parents attended while they were completing their doctoral studies.

Irene was visiting her parents one Sunday when Hans filled in behind the pulpit—only the second time he had preached. His previous attempt had not gone well. Knees knocking, Hans had finished forty minutes of material in half that time. Determined not to make the same mistake again, Hans prepared twice as much content and spoke slowly. He worked verse by verse through sections of Hebrews and provided detailed historical context. He had finished only half his twelve-page outline after forty minutes.

"I loved it," Irene recalled. "As a person who was really dry spiritually, it was a rare occurrence when I was actually learning about the Bible. In most churches I visited, preaching often lacked the gospel of Jesus Christ."

A friendship that began with seminary advice blossomed over the phone as they bonded over a common interest in thoughtful worship. Soon they began a long-distance relationship. Hans shared with Irene a token of his affection—*Religious Affections* by Jonathan Edwards.

What they learned together from Edwards sustained them over the next two years through many difficult conversations. Hans, who attended Central Baptist Theological Seminary, an independent Baptist school, had counseled Irene against studying at Yale. Irene, however, saw God's provision in a full-tuition scholarship. Hans refused to budge, even when he worried she would break up with him.

In *Religious Affections*, Edwards probes our thoughts and behavior to ask: Do you love anything more than God? Hans stuck with his theological convictions rather than trying to please his girlfriend. Irene strived to remain faithful in dialogues and paper writing, even when she disagreed with world-class scholars and gifted classmates.

Edwards would have had it no other way.

About 2,500 people met at Bethlehem Baptist Church in 2003 to mark Jonathan Edwards's three hundredth birthday. The scene must have warmed the heart of J. I. Packer, who spoke to the crowd about Edwards and revival. For more than sixty years the renowned theologian has promoted the Puritans for anyone who would listen. For most of that time few bothered. But during Piper's tenure as pastor of Bethlehem Baptist, he has helped renew popular interest in Edwards. Piper's discovery of joy in the theology of this New England colonial pastor catapulted his ministry.

Edwards has similarly captivated a growing number of evangelicals. Transcendence, transformation, and tradition converge in Edwards. Many young evangelicals have found in Edwards a historical model for Christian commitment. And like all good Puritans, Edwards blows away modern readers with his knowledge of Scripture and his vision for the majesty of God.

"What Edwards saw in God and in the universe because of God, through the lens of Scripture, was breathtaking," Piper explains in *A God-Entranced Vision of All Things: The Legacy of Jonathan Edwards*. "To read him, after you catch your breath, is to breathe the uncommon air of the Himalayas of revelation. And the refreshment that you get from this high, clear, God-entranced air does not take out the valleys of suffering in this world, but fits you to spend your life there for the sake of love with invincible and worshipful joy."[1]

---

[1]John Piper, "A God-Entranced Vision of All Things: Why We Need Jonathan Edwards 300 Years Later," in *A God-Entranced Vision of All Things: The Legacy of Jonathan Edwards*, ed. John Piper and Justin Taylor (Wheaton, IL: Crossway Books, 2004), 22.

Owing much to Piper, there is more interest in Edwards today among evangelicals than any time in at least a hundred and fifty years, according to Doug Sweeney, an Edwards scholar. A church history professor at Trinity Evangelical Divinity School, Sweeney attributes the attraction in part to the pastor-theologian ministry model. Schools like Trinity have renewed the evangelical commitment to learned clergy by equipping them with theological tools for teaching. Those students have one contemporary model in Piper. They find many more models in church history with the Puritans, who outshine most others with teaching depth, zeal for holiness, and high regard for the Bible. With Trinity promoting the pastor-theologian model, it's no coincidence that the number of Calvinists at Trinity has increased in the last twenty years, according to Sweeney.

Interest in Puritan studies has grown at another leading evangelical school, Gordon-Conwell Theological Seminary. Church history professor Garth Rosell said he suspects that young evangelicals gravitate toward the Puritans as they look for deeper historic roots and models for high-commitment Christianity.

That squares with what Jordan Thomas, a twenty-eight-year-old church planter, told me about the Puritans. "I don't read them to find out what these guys say about Calvinism," Thomas said as we talked at Piper's church. "It's their big-hearted love for Christ. They say such things about their devotion to him that I'm just like, *I wonder if I know the same Jesus these guys love.*"

Edwards illustrated his remarkable devotion to God at age nineteen when he wrote down a list of resolutions that he vowed to read each week. The first gives you a taste for the rest: "Resolved, that I will do whatsoever I think to be most to God' s glory." Today youthful interest in Edwards produced the Resolved conference, so named to commemorate and promote Edwards's deliberate lifestyle. Resolved hosted three thousand twenty-something evangelicals in February 2007 and turned away five hundred more on the waiting list. Organizers made plans to host the event in a nine-thousand-seat venue in 2008.

Conference visionary Rick Holland, forty-four, directs student ministries at Grace Community Church, pastored by John MacArthur in Sun Valley, California. Holland wants young evangelicals to emulate Edwards's sanctifying fear of God's holiness and longing for God's beauty. That's a grand goal for a generation that Holland told me "doesn't take anything seriously except for their next hamburger." So why do they like Edwards?

"We have lost a sense of anything transcendent and with *gravitas* in our culture," Holland explained. "This is the *Seinfeld* culture—it's about nothing. Edwards has something to say about what's infinitely important. He discovered in God what was both delightful and disturbing. And the more he investigated the infinite tributaries of God's nature, the more he unearthed his own sinfulness. He began to see the weight of the glory of God, which became the gravity of his life. So he was compelled to respond. That's where the resolutions came from, and that's where his life was set in such a different trajectory than even his peers."

All the glowing things I heard about Edwards made me wonder what had reduced his popular image to fire and brimstone. Sweeney describes his followers as launching "perhaps the most popular movement of indigenous theology in American evangelical history," the New England Theology.[2] So what tarnished his legacy? The answer helps explain why Calvinism declined in America.

Controversy erupted during the first half of the nineteenth century as Edwards loyalists reworked his theology in the rapidly changing, young American republic. Some key Edwards beliefs, such as imputed sin, fell by the wayside. Theologians squabbled over which doctrinal innovations Edwards would endorse.

"[The New England Theology] declined primarily because its leaders had long ago become self-absorbed, expending most of their energy on internal struggles for control of their movement's vast resources," Sweeney writes. "As a result, they failed to respond effectively to the changing needs of the world around them. And, after a while, that changing world just passed them by."[3]

Calvinist titans clashed when Princeton Seminary's Charles Hodge took on Edwards Amasa Park, a chief New England theologian, over the

---

[2]Douglas A. Sweeney, *Nathaniel Taylor, New Haven Theology, and the Legacy of Jonathan Edwards* (New York: Oxford University Press, 2003), 142.
[3]Ibid., 143.

relationship of the intellect and feelings. By the time of their debate in 1850, near the end of the Second Great Awakening, not much Calvinism endured outside their respective traditions—Presbyterianism and Congregationalism. According to historian Mark Noll, Calvinism had pretty much disappeared from Congregationalism by 1900. And Hodge's theological descendants, including B. B. Warfield and J. Gresham Machen, published brilliant theological studies but lost their seminary and their denomination's leadership by 1930.

"Many factors contributed to this decline," Noll writes. "One of them may have been the overly precise scruples and overly sharp scalpels of its [Calvinism's] exponents."[4] In other words, Calvinists don't always play nice, even with each other.

It would take a Harvard atheist to revive interest in Edwards and the Puritans. Perry Miller published his landmark *The New England Mind* in 1939 and lauded Edwards as a philosopher without peer in American history. Ever since, scholars have shown growing interest. Yale University's Jonathan Edwards Center estimates that PhD dissertations about Edwards have doubled in every decade since Miller conceived publishing *The Works of Jonathan Edwards* in 1953.

Evangelicals, oddly enough, have been slower to catch on. Inside the church, most Christians regard Puritans only a little more favorably than do the skeptical masses. That saddens J. I. Packer, who has spent most of his life producing theology in the Puritan tradition. I eagerly anticipated weeks when Packer, a *Christianity Today* senior editor, would fly into Chicago from his home in Vancouver. I snagged every opportunity to take the octogenarian to dinner and probe his mind, which remains as sharp as his eyesight, recently corrected by surgery to give him near-perfect vision. Over spicy-hot Asian food, Packer would advise me on theology articles I wrote or edited or counseled me on whether I should enter pastoral ministry. With Packer you can also expect a healthy dose of sharp British wit. If you're not careful, it might come at your expense. More than a few times I published an article or news section that the eminent theologian found to be a dreadful bore.

---

[4]Mark A. Noll, ed., *The Princeton Theology 1812–1921: Scripture, Science, and Theological Method from Archibald Alexander to Benjamin Breckinridge Warfield* (Grand Rapids, MI: Baker Academic, 2001), 186.

It's not good enough for Packer to publish good theology. The quality of writing must live up to the precious doctrines revealed to us by God in Scripture.

On one occasion Packer and I sat down at the *CT* offices to talk about what the Puritans teach him and how they can help today's church. Packer's personal testimony coincides with the ups and downs of Calvinism on both sides of the Atlantic since World War II. As a junior at Oxford University in 1945, Packer got some big spiritual help from reading John Owen, a British Puritan who preceded Edwards. Packer had become a Christian only one year earlier through the ministry of InterVarsity Christian Fellowship. Owen's treatise on *The Mortification of Sin* helped Packer overcome the sin that entangled him.

For more than six decades since then, Packer has directed others to read the Puritans in order to grow in godliness. Packer and a friend started a conference for studying and promoting Puritan wisdom. They even pulled in Martyn Lloyd-Jones, the famed London preacher of Westminster Chapel, to chair the Westminster Conference, which lasted twenty years without one year off.

"I had the sense in the late forties and early fifties that there was indeed a stirring among the dry bones," Packer recalled. "The evangelical life of Britain was being fertilized in a fresh way by purer Reformed theology—Westminster Confession stuff, Calvin, and Puritan teaching about the Christian life."

However, the sixties saw a new movement of the Holy Spirit. The charismatic renewal emphasized experience and affections—topics important to the Puritans. But this new wave lacked the patience to plunge the depths of Puritan theology.

"Like a tsunami it swept away most of what we thought had been building and growing for more than ten years," Packer said.

Meanwhile in America various streams of Calvinism endured. But Dutch Reformed churches did not fully assimilate into evangelicalism. That limited the influence of scholarship at Calvin Theological Seminary, which dates back to 1876, and that stream of Reformed theology. Presbyterians played key roles in the postwar evangelical surge but still reeled from losing control of Princeton in the early twentieth century. Harold John Ockenga, who helped found the National Association of Evangelicals, had started a degree at Princeton but left the school in 1929 with Machen and others who founded Westminster Theological Seminary in Philadelphia. Against the backdrop of that history, many evangelical leaders spent more energy fighting mainline liberals and fundamentalist separatists than parsing each other's theology.

Meanwhile, the Puritan influence dwindled almost to nothing. During visits to America, Packer often spoke to tiny crowds who gathered for conferences devoted to the Puritans.

"If we had a hundred people, we were lucky," Packer recalled. "We never saw more than two hundred at any of them. So in those days there wasn't any passion in North America for furthering a cause of Puritan theology."

Calvinism certainly did not disappear. Voices here and there powerfully advocated "the doctrines of grace." James Montgomery Boice pastored Tenth Presbyterian Church in Philadelphia and helped set up the Philadelphia Conference on Reformed Theology. That conference, run by the Alliance of Confessing Evangelicals, continues to draw together leading Calvinists for regional events. Roger Nicole, a founding member of the Evangelical Theological Society, taught for years at Gordon-Conwell Theological Seminary. R. C. Sproul, a teaching minister in the Presbyterian Church in America, founded Ligonier Ministries more than thirty-five years ago. Ligonier promotes Reformed theology, in part by reprinting Puritan classics. It would be hard to imagine the response seen today by Piper and other high-profile Reformed teachers apart from the foundation laid over decades by Sproul. A brilliant thinker, clear communicator, and able apologist, Sproul has seen a dramatic increase of interest in Reformed theology as some evangelicals invest more time exploring the character and doctrine of God the Father. "Once they deal with the transcendent majesty of God," Sproul told me, "then they're open to the sovereignty of God and doctrines of grace."

Yale University's Beinecke Rare Book and Manuscript Library would be the answer to the world's easiest game of "one of these things just doesn't belong." The neo-Gothic towers of the law school and imposing columns of the university commons and war memorial surround Beinecke. The modernist library looks like a giant stone egg crate, according to Ken Minkema, executive director of the Jonathan Edwards Center. I met Minkema inside Beinecke to view one of the library's most valuable collections. Yale hosts 90 percent of Edwards's notes and manuscripts.

The papers have held up pretty well over the centuries, even though the library stores them in simple folders. I was surprised that we didn't need gloves to handle the texts. Still, I held the fragile documents with reverential care. Minkema showed me a public oration Edwards delivered upon earning his master's degree from Yale in 1723. One year earlier the college's leaders abandoned Puritanism for their longtime rival, Anglicanism. Petrified Puritans referred to the incident as the "great heresy." Edwards stood in the pulpit of New Haven's Center Church and defended a key Puritan belief, Christ's imputed righteousness.

Next we flipped through his *Miscellaneous Observations on Important Theological Subjects*, with more than fourteen hundred entries during his years at Yale. This was his fruit from studying thirteen hours per day. Edwards wrote in remarkably small font with full script. I could see when thoughts must have rushed through his mind, as he didn't bother to stop for punctuation. Looking at these notes from his early days, you could see the embryonic ideas of a genius who would go on to produce theological masterpieces such as *Freedom of the Will*. Because of his consistent and organized study habits, Edwards completed this project in only ninety days when he finally found time to sit down and write it years later.

The Edwards show-and-tell culminated when I held what Minkema described as the "most known and least read" sermon in American history, "Sinners in the Hands of an Angry God." Edwards first delivered the sermon for his congregation in Northampton, Massachusetts, in June 1741. But the sermon's popularity spread quickly once he preached it the next month in Enfield, Connecticut. The outline I held highlighted the sermon's most memorable passages:

> The God that holds you over the pit of hell, much as one holds a spider . . . abhors you, and is dreadfully provoked. . . . You are ten thousand times more abominable in his eyes than the most hateful venomous serpent is in ours.

Edwards tucked the outline into his jacket when he traveled around New England during the First Great Awakening delivering his on-demand sermon.

> And now, you have an extraordinary opportunity, a day wherein Christ has thrown the door of mercy wide open, and stands in calling and crying with a loud voice to poor sinners; a day wherein many are flocking to him, and pressing into the kingdom of God.[5]

Unlike the "Sinners" outline, Edwards wrote out the farewell address for his longtime congregation in 1750. The man who told the world about revival in Northampton had been fired by his now-famous congregation, which revolted when he changed a long-standing church policy instituted by his grandfather, Solomon Stoddard, the pastor who preceded him. Edwards wanted to reserve Communion for church members who could confess a born-again faith in Jesus Christ. But his grandfather taught the church that Communion would help draw the unconverted toward saving faith. Edwards, a perfectionistic pastor, finally proved too much for the good people of Northampton. Bowed but not broken, Edwards reminded the church in his farewell that one day judgment would come and reveal who was right.

It's hard to convey the excitement of looking through centuries-old notes. But the nearly unintelligible writing gave me a tiny glimpse into the thought life of a singular genius, a foundational evangelical leader of intimidating godliness. The collection took me back to a time when God poured out his Holy Spirit and granted revival across New England. Sadly, time has not been kind to Edwards's cause. The church where Edwards spoke about imputed righteousness in 1723 now advertises its support for alternative sexual lifestyles. The gated, stately buildings on Yale's campus belie the socially progressive academics and students who set the nation's cultural tone.

The past awkwardly collided with the present when Minkema and I walked across campus to Jonathan Edwards College, Yale's first and most prestigious residential college. The close-knit residential colleges offer academic and social support for undergraduates. Students in

---

[5]See http://www.ccel.org/e/edwards/sermons/sinners.html.

Jonathan Edwards College make lighthearted sport of their namesake. Their clothing gear features the college mascot, a spider, or its badge, a tempting apple enveloped by a serpent.

We toured the Jonathan Edwards College master's house, which preserves some of the most valuable Edwards artifacts. We walked down a narrow hallway to see the desk where Edwards studied away his days. Having a classic William and Mary design, the desk included drawers where Edwards stored his Miscellanies. Boxes across the top of the desk stored completed manuscripts. But we didn't see the boxes; they had been removed to make way for two paintings of nude men. On the adjacent wall hung priceless portraits of Jonathan and his wife, Sarah. Jonathan, donning a white wig and traditional cleric's garb, concentrates his stern gaze on an unknown object. Maybe he didn't appreciate the taste in art. I understood why Sarah looked a little flush in the cheeks.

After lunch I walked to Yale Divinity School and the offices of the Jonathan Edwards Center. The center, started in 2003, now oversees the decades-long effort to compile and publish the complete works of Edwards. I sat down with Caleb Maskell, the exceptionally gifted associate director of the center. Just twenty-nine, Caleb speaks with deep awareness of Edwards history alongside an evangelical concern for contemporary religious experience. We talked about why young evangelicals invest serious time and endure brain cramps reading Edwards's sermons and treatises.

"To have Edwards on your shelf—better yet to read him—is to say, 'I want to be deeply connected to the church that has come before. I want my identity to be consistent with the orthodoxy that the church has espoused,'" Caleb explained.

Just as Edwards exemplifies tradition and transcendence with an eye toward transformation, he balances doctrinal conviction with evangelical spirit. During the excitement and chaos of the Great Awakening, Edwards taught his congregation how to discern genuine movements of the Holy Spirit. Even today, his *Religious Affections* strikes the right note. It teaches us how to be emotional without succumbing to emotionalism, how to value doctrine without become doctrinaire.

"People can appropriate Edwards for all sorts of things because he holds together what most people hold apart—doctrine and experience, preaching and revival," Caleb said. "If Edwards has one thing, it's an integrated worldview. And if there's one thing evangelicals of the early twenty-first century—people spun out of seeker-friendly churches—are looking for, it's an integrated worldview."

On the map provided by my New Haven hotel, the building on the corner of State and Grove is St. Boniface's Church. That's also the name etched in stone above the church's front doors. Yet a small sign on the fence next to this church now identifies it as Trinity Baptist Church. A plaque inside the building commemorates the church's dedication on October 22, 2006.

It's safe to say that the kneelers and confessionals get much less use now. The church has dismantled most of the altar, except for the part that runs up the back wall. But I couldn't see much of that part anyway. It was shrouded by a screen that projected the lyrics for contemporary worship music.

Typical of church in a college town, the pews filled out moments before the service started and during the first couple of songs. As many as half of the roughly three hundred in attendance looked about college age. They reflected the New Haven community—Asian, Indian, African-American, but mostly white. The pastors stepped to the podium after five songs led by a small informal choir and string accompaniment. Josh Moody, a thirty-seven-year-old pastor from Great Britain, preached for fifty minutes about "The God-Centered Church." He delivered a firm defense of biblical, traditional models of church practice. But he reminded the congregation that all the right doctrine in the world can't save a heart unaffected by the gospel.

"There's only one thing worse than being heretical in preaching—being boring," Moody said. "We're talking about God here."

A few minutes later he backtracked. Actually, it is better to be boring than heretical, Moody said. Nevertheless, his point stuck. True to his advice, Moody wasn't boring. He joked about planning an evangelistic outreach: "How to Be a Baptist and Not Handle Snakes." He assured the congregation that not all Christians believe in young-earth creationism, speak in a southern accent, or forbid fornication lest it lead to dancing. Thanks to these jokes I picked up a hint about the church's denominational ties. Nowhere in the building could I find any reference to the Southern Baptist Convention. I doubt the church leaders simply forgot.

By the time Moody's sermon ended, I surmised that Trinity Baptist might be the most counterintuitive church in America. A British expatriate leads this Southern Baptist church that meets in a former Roman Catholic church in New Haven, Connecticut. On top of everything else, Moody teaches Reformed theology as he guides this church's rapid growth.

There aren't too many Christians in New Haven, let alone Calvinists, so Moody avoids the label. In any event, it would be more helpful to describe him as an Edwardsian. Moody earned his PhD at Cambridge by writing a dissertation on Edwards. His fascination began as a Cambridge undergrad while he read about the French Enlightenment. In the library, he searched for ammunition to refute the Enlightenment's anti-Christian streams. He picked up a book from the same time period and flipped to a page with a drawing of a spider leaping through the air. Another book by the same author read like the Scripture-soaked sermons of the Puritans. Moody had discovered Jonathan Edwards.

"*Hold on*, I thought, *I've just read what appears to be a very Newton-like piece of scientific investigation*," Moody writes in *The God-Centered Life*, a book that applies Edwards's teaching to contemporary theological issues. "Now, by the same author, I've read a Puritan sermon. This could be it."[6]

And so began a love for Edwards that brought Moody across the Atlantic to pastor a church in New Haven. After the morning worship service, Moody and I walked down the street and settled in a pub. Listening to his accent, we might have been on the British Isles. I shared with Moody my fascination with his unique church. I pointed out the peculiar juxtaposition of the projection screen and altar. "We call that the white castle," Moody said. They planned to remove the altar as

[6]Josh Moody, *The God-Centered Life: Insights from Jonathan Edwards for Today* (Vancouver, BC: Regent College Publishing, 2007), 17.

soon as a professional could arrive and carefully dismantle the parts. "We like to think of this as the Reformation all over again."

That apt analogy had eluded me. In parts of Europe, including England, Protestants met after the schism in the same buildings where Christians had gathered for centuries as Roman Catholics. Radical Puritans spared nothing when they converted church buildings.

When I asked Moody about how he landed at Trinity Baptist, he shared a story to match his peculiar church. He explained that Yale Divinity School students started the congregation as New Haven Fellowship of Christ in the 1970s. But the fledgling church struggled to pay its bills. Giving from Yale students fell short. So in the 1980s the church, under the name of Trinity Baptist Church, moved to a nearby suburb. The move failed because the church no longer attracted many students. Divisions among the members eventually split the church. Maybe that was inevitable—the church never composed a doctrinal statement, so theological views ran the gamut.

A small but determined group from one of the splits moved back into New Haven. For ten years they searched for a pastor without success. They came within hours of giving up. The few remaining members met to shut down Trinity Baptist the same day they first heard about Moody. Someone on the pastoral search committee heard about a nearby church that rejected Moody for being too evangelical. Trinity Baptist Church issued a call to Moody and his wife.

"We said yes, never having met anyone in the church," Moody recalled. "We flew out three weeks later with a laptop, printer, and three suitcases. The first time I met any of the members was when I was preaching to them the first Sunday."

Trinity Baptist Church had dwindled to fewer than thirty members when they called Moody in 1999. At the beginning of 2006 they counted nearly three hundred members. The congregation took a giant step forward by purchasing the church from the Roman Catholic diocese after outgrowing rented space.

Through Moody, Edwards continues to influence Yale students. Moody believes that Edwards communicates to Christians today in ways they may not have appreciated a few decades ago. Postmodernism has raised concerns about the balance of reason and emotion, sense and sensibility, scientific and romantic worldviews.

"We're living culturally in a time that's reassessing if not abandoning our Enlightenment heritage," Moody said. "It's taken us two hundred years to realize, as Edwards did, that we should not be bowled over by the Enlightenment. He accepted some of the Enlightenment and rejected other parts of it. Likewise, we should be neither modernists nor postmodernists. We should reject parts of each. I think Edwards helps us with that, particularly with issues of the emotions. He does really good surgery on the heart and mind."

As much as I enjoy reading Edwards, I told Moody that I doubt we'll ever again see his writing reach the bulk of evangelicals, as it did during the Great Awakening. My marked-up copy of *Religious Affections* runs nearly four hundred pages in the Banner of Truth version. And that's one of his more accessible works. I haven't yet dared to pick up *Freedom of the Will.*

"Even if reading Edwards makes someone think, *This is too much for me*, I'm quite glad it does, because it makes them feel there's something they should be shooting for that's a little more profound than cheesy Christianity," Moody said. "It's like taking someone who wants to run the 100-meter dash for school to see an Olympic sprinter."

That's both the genius and the problem with Edwards. Sometimes I think about how exciting it must have been to hear Edwards preach week after week in Northampton. But would I have wanted Edwards as my pastor? It's one thing to read *Religious Affections*, quite another to expect counsel and care from my pastor. Studying thirteen hours each day didn't leave much time for pastoral visits.

"He had a very high IQ," Moody said. "But I'm not sure he had high EQ [emotional intelligence]. There are some things he could have done differently and saved a lot of hassle for a lot of people."

Unfortunately, this man who understood Christian experience like few others struggled at times to relate to his congregation. When the Communion controversy flared, Edwards responded with page after page of theological justification. The church was in no mood for another lecture. But what else could he do? Over the years he became aloof, disconnected from the personal relationships that might have persuaded the church to give him the benefit of the doubt.

"A gentle answer turns away wrath, and a patient word can break a bone," Moody writes, "but lengthy treatises, however brilliant and sparkling with intellectual insight, are likely to be a turn off unless first the groundwork of agreement has been laid more personally and privately."[7]

If some young Calvinists give Piper undue reverence, the temptation to idolize Edwards might be stronger. It's easy to rip Edwards out of historical context and ignore the more challenging aspects of his character. That goes for any effort by young evangelicals to learn from and honor church tradition. Christians must seek not a return to the Reformation or the First Great Awakening but a return to Jesus Christ, the founder and perfecter of our faith.

I'm no fan of ghost stories, and I certainly don't enjoy feeling like I'm the unwitting subject of one. But after dark on Yale's campus, surrounded by daunting stone structures, that might not be a unique experience. I knew that Reformed University Fellowship (RUF) meets in the common room of Dwight Hall, one of the campus's oldest buildings. Still, as I felt my way through the dark in the adjacent chapel, I saw no signs of an upcoming meeting. I was a little early, but not too early. Once I finally found the light switch, my fear abated only a little. The chapel likely hasn't changed in decades, if not more than a century. A high-arching ceiling and sturdy stone pillars make the chapel seem like it could seat hundreds. Yet fewer than one hundred chairs ran the length of the chapel. I saw no signs of life. I walked outside, just in case I had the wrong location. Across the road I saw a building conspicuous in its attempt to be discreet. A map confirmed what I suspected—that was the famed Skull and Bones secret society's tomb, an apt description for the building.

Back in Dwight Hall, I settled in the common room, which lacks the crypt-like charm of the chapel. Similarly timeless, the room felt quite plain, even a little bit dingy. But we're talking about Yale here. Dingy conveys history. Dwight Hall, the old library, stands as a reminder of a

---

[7] Ibid., 148.

little-known period of the university's past. The building's namesake, Timothy Dwight, saw revival transform Yale during his tenure as university president from 1795–1817. You might say revival ran in his family—his grandfather was Jonathan Edwards.

Any lingering anxiety I felt finally lifted when a couple of RUF leaders arrived. Eventually seventeen students showed up for the meeting, which began with hymns suitable for accompaniment by acoustic guitar, such as "Be Thou My Vision." RUF prefers this approach to the amped-up performances that kick off other college groups. That's just one unique characteristic of RUF, the college ministry of the Presbyterian Church in America. RUF also carves out a niche by embracing Christian tradition and intellectual depth. Of course, RUF loses the academic distinction at Yale. That's not the group's only struggle to stand out.

"Some people think we're a Jewish group," said Daniel Thies, the president of RUF at Yale. "Your average Yalies don't have the term *Reformed* in their vocabulary."

Following announcements, including a pitch for a winter retreat planned for Cape Cod, Clay Daniel stood up to preach. The RUF campus minister spoke on "Something to Live for: The Urgency of Joy," drawn from the parable in Matthew 13 where Jesus talks about abandoning everything for the kingdom of heaven.

"The kingdom of heaven centers on the rule of God himself," Clay, thirty-one, said. "That is where the joy is found. The Bible depicts God's reign as a joyous reign. When God rules over his people, his actions are an overflow of the joy of his heart, the joy of creating a people for himself, for his own glory, and blessing them measure upon measure."

The sermon did not seem especially tweaked for undergraduates. He did, however, warn the students against hedonism and ambition. "Jesus himself entered into the joy of the kingdom so that we might turn from our pathetic autonomy and lusting after joy and turn to the rightful object of all our affections." Sounds like Edwards for the twenty-first century.

It's no coincidence that so many Christian ministries—Passion, Campus Crusade for Christ, InterVarsity Christian Fellowship, and so on—target college students. They're old enough to comprehend complex topics and make life-defining decisions, but not so old that they are set in their beliefs. For many, it's their first time away from home, an opportunity to try new things. The same tumult that makes Christian parents fear college also provides a tremendous opportunity for evangelism.

College was one of the first turning points in young Jonathan Edwards's life. He experienced a dramatic new "sense of the glory of the divine being" during his time at Yale.[8] Only thirteen when he started, Edwards was uncommonly mature and complained about rabble-rousing students. Edwards spent his time wrestling with weighty theological questions. The historical figure most closely associated today with reviving the doctrines of grace himself agonized over the "horrible doctrine" that the sovereign God would leave some to suffer eternal torment in hell. But once he submitted to the biblical portrait of God's justice, Edwards expressed "how happy I should be, if I might enjoy that God, and be wrapped up to God in heaven, and be as it were swallowed up in him."[9]

I tagged along with RUF to learn about the Reformed approach to college ministry. RUF at Yale might be a unique case. One of the smaller ministries at Yale, RUF attracts a unique blend of students. Some had become Christians recently. Others just want to learn more about Christianity before they commit to anything. With a more traditional Protestant feel, RUF at Yale attracts some students who grew up in confessional churches, even from liberal denominations. They know only a little more about Edwards than average Yale undergrads. But if they stick with RUF, they're sure to get a heavy dose of Reformed theology, starting with the Westminster Confession.

Clay Daniel began with RUF at Yale in 2003. So he felt a special attachment to the 2007 graduating class, the first group he watched grow from freshmen to seniors. We talked about what makes RUF special and how the ministry has affected the broader Reformed world. Growing up in Virginia's Shenandoah Valley, Clay attended a Presbyterian church, but of the mainline variety. Church did not really influence his spiritual life. His high school and college years tell

---

[8]Quoted in George M. Marsden, *Jonathan Edwards: A Life* (New Haven, CT: Yale University Press, 2003), 41.
[9]Quoted in ibid., 41.

the great American evangelical story. Active with Young Life in high school, Clay connected with Campus Crusade for Christ at Harvard. He even spent a summer sharing the gospel in Paris on a Crusade summer project. For a time he attended historic Park Street Church in Boston. But he also bounced around and dabbled with a Vineyard congregation and a Korean Presbyterian church. He didn't attend any of these churches regularly.

"I wasn't that big on the church," Clay admitted. "I felt like going to church was important, but I didn't see it as the very center of my spiritual life."

Despite his hesitation about church, Clay took his first job after Harvard as the youth director of a United Methodist church back in Virginia. But soon he moved on to new challenges. He began looking for a seminary. Fed up with New England, he crossed Gordon-Conwell off his list. Trinity Evangelical Divinity School was too expensive. After an extensive, thoughtful search process, he settled on Dallas Theological Seminary. Dallas even put him near his beloved Dallas Cowboys football team. So he and his wife packed their bags for Texas.

Somehow, by attending a predominantly Baptist independent seminary, Clay reconnected with his Presbyterian roots. A number of his seminary friends attended Park Cities Presbyterian Church, a major PCA congregation. The church attracted him with liturgy and Word-centered preaching.

"Instead of leaving the service with things to do, I was thinking about something to believe," Clay said. "The services were centered on God's Word. We worshiped with reverence and awe, focused on God's story of redemption—not mostly our story with God's rules intersecting at certain places. The panorama of God's redemption was being painted for me."

TULIP did not draw him back into the Reformed tradition. Actually, Clay had been sympathetic to Calvinism in college. But he considered the Calvinists he knew to be "a little wacky" for pushing what he considered to be minor theological points. The Reformed perspective no longer seemed so minor when he began to understand covenant theology, how God's story of redemption unfolds across the Old and New Testaments in the covenants of works, redemption, and grace. This directly contradicted the theology he picked up from classes at Dallas, the epicenter of covenant theology's great rival, dispensationalism. Unlike covenant theology, dispensationalism stresses God's enduring purposes for Israel and interprets redemptive history as a series of ages when God deals differently with his image-bearers.

En route to better understanding Reformed theology, Clay stumbled over baptism. Despite his Presbyterian upbringing, Clay morphed into a nominal Baptist through the influence of parachurch ministries. The PCA—like most Reformed churches—practices infant baptism. After he began to understand the big picture of God's redemptive plan, Clay changed his mind. "Infant baptism only made sense as the tip of the iceberg resting on the weighty foundation of the covenantal system," he explained.

That wasn't Clay's only major shift. His involvement with Park Cities also changed his mind about the centrality of the local church. He began to see church as the center of his spiritual life. And that made him a perfect fit for church-centered RUF when he decided to head back to the Ivy League as a campus minister. Within the Ivy League, RUF also operates at Harvard and Brown. The Brown chapter had grown so large, with around a hundred and fifty students, that the administration singled out RUF with spurious claims and suspended it in fall 2006 for a few months.

Nationwide, RUF has increased from thirty-five campuses in 1998 to more than one hundred today. In more than two decades as the PCA college ministry, RUF has fed the growing denomination with an exuberant generation of pastors who have gained invaluable experience as college ministers in evangelism, discipleship, and preaching. It's common for PCA church planters to cut their teeth with RUF. Their energy has leavened the PCA.

"A lot of this desire to keep the joy and vibrancy of Reformed faith in the PCA has come through RUF," said George Levesque, Yale's dean of freshman affairs and an elder with Christ Presbyterian Church, which sponsors RUF at Yale.

RUF's strength is one reason the PCA continues to grow even as so many denominations stagnate or decline. First Presbyterian Church in Jackson, Mississippi, helped launch RUF decades ago. Its pastor, Ligon

Duncan, told me that RUF's ties to local Presbyterian churches help students become exceptional church members and leaders after they graduate. RUF has trained them to expect expositional preaching alongside serious evangelistic efforts. RUF thrives on many southern campuses, welcoming a number of Baptist refugees. Duncan said Adrian Rogers, the late architect of the Southern Baptist Convention's conservative resurgence, once called the local RUF leader into his Memphis office to ask what so many of his Baptist students found appealing about the PCA.

"You get all of these evangelical kids whose instincts are right but who have not been taught in their churches," Duncan said. "And suddenly they encounter an RUF large group where somebody is intelligent but overtly and unapologetically Christian and confessional and theological and expositional. And it's like the moth to the flame." Duncan, I should note, did not attempt to hide his glee.

Duncan confirmed what I heard from Clay about the appeal of traditional worship. Hymns in PCA churches might seem wholly different from the modern rock at Passion conferences. Yet whether you're reciting historic creeds or belting out God-centered praise choruses, you proclaim the transcendent God. Liturgy may have grown stale for their parents, but the young evangelicals turning to RUF and the PCA worship as they lose themselves in tradition.

"Among the twenty- and thirty-somethings who show up at my church there is a desire for an approach to worship that is more formal, historical, and transcendent than they have experienced in the church settings they're coming from," said Duncan, forty-six. "Not among my boomers. My boomers would love for us to do whatever they're doing in the megachurches in Chicago or Minneapolis or Los Angeles. But not the young ones."

They might have enjoyed a certain church in Northampton, Massachusetts.

CHAPTER FOUR

Ground Zero

SOUTHERN BAPTIST THEOLOGICAL SEMINARY

LOUISVILLE, KENTUCKY

It's a good thing I waited to visit Southern Baptist Theological Seminary until after I decided to attend another seminary. Because if I had visited Southern first, I don't think I could have resisted the temptation to commit on the spot just based on the scenery. On a sunny late May afternoon I couldn't stand to do all my interviews inside. So I coaxed Matt Hall into giving me a brief tour around the campus, situated in a leafy, lazy section of Louisville. I met Matt, a twenty-seven-year-old former Southern student, in the foyer of Norton Hall. The striking campus centerpiece resembles the stately red-brick churches that Southern's graduates will pastor. It's the kind of academic building that looks perfect on a sentimental appeal for alumni donations.

We headed outside and walked to the Honeycutt Campus Center, a vibrant student facility more suited to undergraduate fun than seminary studies. Thanks to its namesake, the Honeycutt Center also reminds students of the president whose retirement in the early 1990s unleashed a controversy that would nearly kill the seminary. Yet Al Mohler, Honeycutt's successor, has guided Southern from the brink of destruction to its current flourishing state—it is the Southern Baptist Convention's largest seminary.

Inside Honeycutt, Matt showed me around the campus bookstore. Here the seminary's unique character became most apparent. Right away I noticed a prominent display of John MacArthur commentaries. The noted Calvinist expositor does not belong to the SBC. Nearby, copies of *By His Grace and For His Glory* were piled up on a table. Written by Southern Seminary history professor Tom Nettles, this book stirred Calvinists to defend their theology with appeals to SBC founders.

Finally, we headed back to Norton Hall and walked to the second floor, where we could find a room to talk. With the building abandoned before Memorial Day, we lingered in Mohler's receiving room. He had invested good money to renovate this part of the building a few years ago. When contrasted with John Piper's home and Bethlehem Baptist Church, I understand why Piper can't let a visit to Southern go by without warning against the comfort encouraged by the seminary's relative opulence. Prominent portraits of famed London pastor Charles Spurgeon and the first Southern president, James P. Boyce, hung on the wall. One day, when Mohler is gone, he may look down from that wall on Southern's next president.

Done with the receiving room, we slipped back into the new studio where Mohler records his daily radio show. Matt now works for Salem Communications, which distributes the program to sixty-two stations nationwide. Mohler is many things to many people—champion of inerrancy who cleared house at Southern, advocate for Calvinism, bibliophile known for untiring work habits. But most know him as a conservative commentator who pops up frequently on CNN with Larry King or on the *Washington Post* web site offering his opinions about breaking news.

Matt makes Mohler's radio program happen. But Southern once seemed an unlikely destination for Matt. A missionary kid, Matt grew up giving top priority to evangelism and considered theology to be divisive. Why bother with theology, Matt figured, because we'll never figure out most debated issues anyway.

College courses gently challenged Matt's assumptions. He took a class on Luther and Calvin at Grove City College and loved it. Their thoughtfulness impressed him. Through their writing he felt like he could experience momentous historical changes. The great Reformers even won him over to their belief that God sovereignly elects his church. Still, Matt's upbringing in seeker-sensitive churches made him wary of labels such as Calvinism. He associated the term with the "frozen chosen."

His reluctance only receded later in college. During the summer of 2001, Matt interned at a large nondenominational church in the Pittsburgh area. The staff asked him to start a ministry for college students and young adults. Searching on the Web for appropriate music, he stumbled upon Passion. He liked what he heard. Through a connection he even arranged for his church to host Louie Giglio on a Passion tour. Giglio's passion for the glory of God struck a nerve with Matt. Giglio cast a vision bigger than what Matt heard in sermons, which had titles like "Seven Easy Ways to Minimize Stress in Your Life." Through Passion, Matt also learned about Piper. He returned to the Web and found endless Piper resources on the Desiring God web site. Matt devoured *The Pleasures of God*, in which Piper describes God's delight in his own glory.

After college Matt prepared to pursue his ministry calling in seminary. A pastor friend recommended Southern. Matt had never heard of Mohler, but he loved the combination of Baptist Calvinism. The gamble paid off. Done with two master's degrees, Matt is now pursuing a PhD in American religious history.

Yet as Matt's views continued to change at Southern, he learned to avoid discussions about Calvinism with his pastor dad. It's not so much the theology his father worries about. It's the implications. Matt began airing his growing concerns about other evangelical theologies when he started blogging in 2003. Not long before I sat down with Matt, he talked with his dad about the critiques posted on his blog. His dad reminded him to balance his passion for biblical truth with a gracious spirit.

"A different generation of evangelicals that includes my dad is not as concerned about my theology," Matt said. "But they would perceive my criticism of elements within evangelicalism as damaging to the cause."

In order to understand why this might be, you need to know a little "history." After World War II, Southern Baptists such as Billy Graham and Carl Henry encouraged evangelicals to engage culture with their conservative theology. Graham preached to presidents and music stars. Henry issued a stirring call with his book *The Uneasy Conscience of Modern Fundamentalism*. They published a magazine together (*Christianity Today*). These leaders believed their third way would prove more faithful than that of the liberals, more fruitful than that of the fundamentalists. In many ways, their plan worked. Their success has afforded today's up-and-coming evangelicals a measure of theological introspection. But elder generations don't always appreciate or understand the resulting self-criticism.

R. Albert Mohler Jr. was too young to head the Southern Baptist Theological Seminary. He thought so. Everyone thought so. Well, not everyone. The board was impressed by his vitality and plan to restore the seminary's confessional identity. During his first convocation as president in 1993, Mohler—thirty-three years old at the time—addressed students and faculty with a talk entitled "Don't Just Do Something: Stand There!" They soon learned what the board saw in Mohler. Not prone to ambiguity, Mohler let the faculty know where he stood by quoting James P. Boyce: "It is no hardship to those who teach here to be called upon to sign the declaration of their principles, for there are fields of usefulness open elsewhere to every man, and none need accept your call who cannot conscientiously sign your formulary."

When Mohler stepped into that chapel pulpit, nearly the entire faculty opposed his agenda. They had good reason to fear him. The board tapped Mohler to bring the conservative resurgence to Southern, which at that point still harbored moderate and liberal professors who didn't endorse the denomination's inerrancy litmus test. No more of that with Mohler in charge. No less than 96 percent of the seminary's faculty left when Mohler took over and solidified his authority with the trustees' backing. Not that many of the faculty had a choice.

"I said, in sum, if this is what you believe, then we want you to stay. If not, then you have come here under false pretenses, and you must go," Mohler, now forty-eight, said. "As they would say, the battle was joined."

What a battle it would be. Southern, nearly a hundred and fifty years old, has been a vital part of Louisville's church life. Mohler faced not only a hostile faculty but an embittered city, including Southern graduates who filled the city's pulpits. To this day he had best avoid some Louisville churches. Television cameras once hindered him from entering his office. News helicopters drowned out telephone conversations. Students camped outside his office singing, "We Shall Overcome." Candlelight vigils carried on live television protested Mohler's leadership.

All this because he reenforced Southern's Abstract of Principles, derived via the Second London Confession from that landmark Reformed document, the Westminster Confession. Due mostly to this foundation, Mohler saw that the seminary had a "heritage to be reclaimed, and I felt a deep personal commitment to that heritage." Indeed, Mohler earned his MDiv and PhD from Southern. However, back then he identified with Southern's liberal wing for a time. Needless to say, something changed.

"One would have to have a providential understanding of history to look back to 1993 and see the events that brought about my election as president and what that might have meant for the future of one part of evangelicalism," Mohler said.

But some of Mohler's inerrancy allies might not have fully foreseen one small twist. Mohler's fidelity to the Abstract of Principles has steered the seminary back toward Calvinism. On providence, the abstract reads, "God from eternity, decrees or permits all things that come to pass, and perpetually upholds, directs and governs all creatures and all events."

God elects without condition, the abstract says. "Election is God's eternal choice of some persons unto everlasting life—not because of foreseen merit in them, but of his mere mercy in Christ." Sovereign grace overcomes human resistance. "Regeneration is a change of heart, wrought by the Holy Spirit, who quickeneth the dead in trespasses and sins enlightening their minds spiritually and savingly to understand the Word of God and renewing their whole nature, so that they love and practice holiness. It is a work of God's free and special grace alone."

When Mohler asked Southern's faculty to teach according to the abstract, the seminary nearly collapsed. Less than fifteen years later, Mohler has attracted one of the strongest evangelical faculties in the country. Though only one of six denominational seminaries, one in four SBC seminarians attends Southern. Southern administrators happily point out that their seminary charges a fraction of what similar seminaries collect in tuition and fees. Enrollment has surged to more than 4,300 students—which makes Southern the largest Southern Baptist seminary, likely the largest U.S. seminary period. Many of these graduates will take Calvinism to pulpits throughout the SBC.

Not that Mohler would suppose that he can or should Calvinize the Convention. When hired at Southern, Mohler dealt with critics who opposed not only his views on election but also his belief in a literal resurrection. The denomination did and does have bigger problems than Calvinism. Mohler may get another platform to address these issues as an announced candidate for SBC president in 2008.

"When I say that my agenda is not Calvinism, I say that with unfeigned honesty, with undiluted candor," Mohler told me. "My agenda is the gospel. And I refuse to limit that to a label, but I am also very honest to say, yes, that means I am a five-point Calvinist. If you're counting points, here I am."

Such a profession hardly placates Mohler's critics. In today's SBC, even honesty is controversial.

Neither side trusts a 2006 survey from LifeWay Research indicating that 10 percent of SBC pastors consider themselves to be five-point Calvinists. Non-Calvinists think even that number is exaggerated. Calvinists believe they claim a larger percentage.

Indeed, a November 2007 Lifeway Study showed that nearly 30 percent of SBC seminary graduates between 1998 and 2004, now serving as pastors, describe themselves as Calvinists.

Today's trends recall the convention's origins. For much of the SBC's formative years, Calvinists did claim a sizable following. Evidence from the Convention's early years points to Calvinist near-dominance. Most early American Baptists took after England's Particular Baptists, so named because they believed in particular redemption, also known as limited atonement. The Calvinists in New England may have exiled Roger Williams, a Baptist, but the founder of Rhode Island shared their views on election.

To learn more about Southern Baptist history, I went straight to one of the top sources. I met Tom Nettles, Southern Seminary professor of historical theology, in downtown Louisville and talked over plates of hot brown. I struggled to finish this filling, tasty Louisville treat, which as far as I could tell consisted of hot turkey suffocated by layers of cheese. Nettles labored through a vicious cold to recap the history recounted in his 1986 book, *By His Grace and for His Glory: A Historical, Theological, and Practical Study of the Doctrines of Grace in Baptist Life.*

In his study of Southern Baptist history, Nettles discovered that Calvinism typified the Convention's written record from its founding in 1845 through the first decade of the twentieth century. America's first published Baptist theologian, John L. Dagg, taught the doctrines of grace. The same goes for James P. Boyce, the Princeton-trained founder and first president of Southern Seminary. "I wrote the book as a personal exercise of convincing myself that I was not off my rocker," Nettles said. But that's exactly what some others think of Nettles. Calvinism cost Nettles a previous job at Mid-American Baptist Seminary.

Southern Baptists crept closer to their modern-day reputation during the tenure of E. Y. Mullins, president of Southern Seminary from 1899 to 1928. Mullins distrusted theological confessions. For many years, Southern Baptists have rallied around the call for "no creed but the Bible, no cause but Christ."

Calvinism began to be seen as too systematic, as if it imposed a foreign meaning on the biblical text. But the decreasing reliance on confessions also allowed liberalism to develop within the Convention. Individualism encouraged by Mullins's anti-confessional approach undermined SBC unity, according to Nettles. Hence the need for a conservative resurgence, which began in 1979 with non-Calvinists such as Adrian Rogers maneuvering to oust leaders who would not affirm biblical inerrancy.

"They had to fight like mad just to keep their head above water on the authority of Scripture," Nettles said. "They didn't have time to develop a systematic theology."

They also needed to find conservatives to fill all the positions opening in seminaries. Calvinists, with their strong inerrancy credentials, emerged as leading candidates. The chief example was Al Mohler at Southern Seminary.

"I saw his selection as providential," Nettles said. "I saw it as something that could not be generated by any human instrument. God himself was doing something that we could never have thought of twenty years ago."

Mohler has silenced critics who said he could never find a first-class faculty to affirm inerrancy. Now it's not ridiculous to think that if Mohler leads Southern as long as Mullins did, he might leave behind the opposite theological legacy.

That's precisely what many in the Convention today fear. As early as 1997 Southern Baptist historian William Estep warned, "If the Calvinizing of Southern Baptists continues unabated, we are in danger of becoming 'a perfect dunghill' in American society." Estep's warning does not seem to have produced the intended effect. Numerous web sites run by Calvinists have reproduced his article as Exhibit A in the war against Calvinists. Forgive them if they feel a little defensive. Estep also wrote, "Calvinism's God resembles Allah, the god of Islam, more than the God of grace and redeeming love revealed in Jesus Christ."[1]

The alarm has been sounded. Could today's debates over Calvinism help unleash a battle that will make the conservative resurgence seem like a skirmish? Malcom Yarnell, assistant dean for theological studies at Southwestern Seminary, seems to think so. "The Controversy or Conservative Resurgence of the late 20th century is a mere precursor to the battles for theological integrity which face us, some of which will make that episode look like child's play."[2]

Mohler himself hinted at rough water ahead in his famous first convocation as Southern president. Inerrancy will give way to bigger controversies, he said. Mohler warned that the SBC was flirting with forfeiting its theological heritage. The Calvinism debate presages the trouble unleashed when modern-day Southern Baptists confront confessionalism of any sort.

"This crisis far outweighs the [inerrancy] controversy that had marked the Southern Baptist Convention for the last fourteen years," Mohler said. "That controversy is a symptom rather than the root cause. As Southern Baptists, we are in danger of becoming God's most

---

[1]William R. Estep, "Doctrines Lead to 'Dunghill,' Prof Warns," *The Founders Journal*, Summer 1997; http://www.founders.org/FJ29/article1.html.
[2]Malcolm B. Yarnell III, "The Heart of a Baptist," White Paper 2 (Fort Worth: Center for Theological Research, December 2005); http://www.baptisttheology.org/documents/TheHeartofaBaptist_001.pdf.

unembarrassed pragmatists—much more enamored with statistics than invested with theological substance."

The question is whether Southern Baptists can weather their intramural fights without weakening each other so much that they encourage a liberal relapse. But that's a risk worth taking for some frustrated Southern Baptists.

"The conservatives have been in charge now for a couple of decades, and our convention is no better off on basic issues than when the liberals were running things," said Tom Ascol, pastor of Grace Baptist Church in Cape Coral, Florida. He also serves as executive director of Founders Ministries, launched in 1982 to reform local churches through a return to the Convention's Calvinist roots. "That's because inerrancy isn't enough. We have to actually understand and apply what the Bible says. The conservatives thump the Bible but are unwilling to just obey the Bible in the most basic ways. How can you be an inerrantist and not practice [church discipline according to] Matthew 18? You might as well be a liberal. What difference does it make?"

For someone who says he doesn't want to stir controversies, Timmy Brister often finds himself in the middle of them. His blog writing doesn't endear him to the executives at Southern Seminary, where he is preparing for pastoral ministry. He gives seminary leaders an earful when they welcome chapel speakers who have elsewhere derided Calvinism.

"It bothers me that I get reprimanded for doing the very thing I'm taught to do," said Timmy, twenty-eight.

I was glad to catch Timmy in the morning when he didn't have to work. He works third shift for UPS in Louisville so he can get to know college students and share the gospel. We enjoyed a spirited chat about his eventful life so far with the SBC. One half of Timmy's family background marks him as an SBC lifer. His grandfather graduated from Southern Seminary in 1943, and his dad joined the Baptist Student Union at Ole Miss. That's where one half met the other half of his family. That side is a whole other story. His Assyrian mother fled Iran after her father died in a car accident and could no longer defend their Christian enclave.

Far from the troubles of revolutionary Iran, Timmy grew up as a jock in Athens, Alabama. He still looks like he could play a smooth shortstop. Before college he had never read any book but the Bible. But boy, did he love reading the Bible. Timmy's passions make sense when he describes the biggest influence on his life, an elderly man who led his Bible study in high school. The man who generously shared his time with Timmy died of a heart attack while preaching in prison.

By that time Timmy had moved to south Alabama to attend the University of Mobile. He chose Mobile over another Baptist school, Samford University in Birmingham, because Samford sided with the moderates who opposed the conservative resurgence. At Mobile, Timmy encountered a strong Reformed movement. But like so many others, he didn't find much appealing about these Calvinists. They told him God would never use him unless he embraced five-point Calvinism, Timmy remembered.

"I looked around at these guys, and I just noticed that they didn't have that same passion," Timmy said. "Even though I didn't have the theology and head knowledge they had, they didn't have the heart that I had."

Circumstances nudged Timmy toward Reformed theology. He was fired from his first church internship, working for an SBC church in Mobile that ranked among the state leaders in baptisms. The pastors there took the CEO ministry model a little too literally, according to Timmy. They spent work hours day-trading stocks, he said. So he wasn't happy when the pastors refused to approve a modest budget he proposed for college ministry. Timmy managed to obtain a copy of the church budget and confronted the staff about their expensive pet projects. Two pastors sat him down for three hours to express their displeasure.

"They called me Absalom," he said, referring to King David's rebellious son. "They told me that I was a no-good, unprofitable servant, that God would never use me in ministry, and that I was a waste of their time and that I could no longer come back to that church." This scenario would sound ridiculous if I hadn't heard similar stories off the record from other young Southern Baptist pastors.

After his first ministry experience, Timmy was pretty sure he wanted nothing to do with churches. He wanted to die anonymously on the mission field. That option sounded especially appealing when his fiancée broke off their engagement and told Timmy she had been cheating on him.

"So the love of my life and my love for the church, the two biggest things in my life, were completely rocked," Timmy said. "I felt like every foundation on which I stood was broken, and all I had left to stand on was what I knew to be true—my Savior, my God, and his control of my life."

God graciously provided sweet fellowship through the Word and the Holy Spirit's comfort in his brokenness. Around this same time Timmy started reading about Reformed theology. He heard Piper speak in 2000 at a Christmas conference for Campus Outreach. Timmy has practically memorized Piper's four messages after listening to each one at least fifty times. In one address Piper taught about enjoying God through suffering and giving your life in service to him. After that conference Timmy began devouring Piper's books and other Calvinist works.

Timmy moved closer to home after college and began working in student ministry for a church. Just twenty-one years old, Timmy bought a house and planned to live the rest of his life there. But during his fourth year Timmy led a staff devotional by reading from Piper's *Brothers, We Are Not Professionals*. The staff didn't appreciate what Timmy implied by reading from Piper's critique of a professional view of pastoral ministry. Timmy said he just wanted to warn them based on his Mobile experience. Still, Timmy did see some parallels. If I had tried to reach him by phone at that three-hundred-member church, Timmy said, I would have first spoken with two secretaries and one intern before I ever caught him. So maybe the devotional hit a little too close to home. The church suspended Timmy for one week without pay. At that point Timmy decided he needed to go to seminary. Timmy expects to either plant his own SBC church or join a Calvinist pastoral staff when he graduates.

Church planting might be the best way to avoid the "tumultuous days" ahead, warned about in 2006 by SBC president Frank Page. Page observed that hundreds of Calvinists graduating from SBC seminaries

have to find jobs somewhere. But if Timmy's experience is any indi-
cation, some Southern Baptist churches have problems greater than
Calvinism.

Nearly every Southern Baptist source I reached on both sides of
the Calvinism debate cited Dauphin Way Baptist Church in Mobile,
Alabama. This venerable church has hosted three SBC presidents in
more than one hundred years. Maybe that's why Steve Lawson was an
odd choice to pastor Dauphin Way. When church leaders came calling,
Lawson pastored a small, nondenominational Bible church in Little
Rock, Arkansas. But they heard from the Billy Graham Evangelistic
Association, which often employed Lawson to train pastors, that he
would admirably fill their pulpit for a week as they searched for a lead
pastor. Once Lawson preached as a guest, church leaders didn't want
him to leave. They observed his considerable gift for expository preaching, the likes of which they hadn't seen since Jerry Vines, one of the
SBC presidents who once filled their pulpit.

Before he answered the call, Lawson wanted to clear his conscience
about one potential problem. He asked church leaders what they
believed about predestination. According to Lawson, they told him they
had never heard a sermon about predestination. He briefly explained
to the leaders his own view, commonly associated with Calvinism,
but he used only biblical terms. Still, the church might have discerned
his allegiances since he earned his DMin from Reformed Theological
Seminary. Lawson said the pulpit committee indicated they would like
to hear him preach about predestination sometime.

Maybe Dauphin Way should have stuck to the SBC farm system.
After Lawson moved to Mobile in 1995, he waited two years before he
preached about God's sovereignty. Despite the committee's initial reaction, he figured the doctrines of grace might not go down smoothly
with Dauphin Way.

"I could've said a word in Russian they could have more quickly
understood than *Calvinism*," Lawson told me. "Their biblical literacy
was amazingly low. Many people weren't even bringing Bibles to
church."

Lawson had problems at Dauphin Way from the get-go. Within

those first two years, one group left Dauphin Way to start its own church. He attributed this first fissure to his expository preaching. The proclaimed Word exposed hearts, he said. It revealed that some church leaders didn't believe what they claimed. Lawson told me about one sixty-five-year-old deacon who approached him privately and asked how he could be saved. According to Lawson, nearly one hundred adult church members professed faith for the first time during his eight-year tenure.

Only his commitment to those adult converts kept him from resigning much earlier during a series of contentious fights, Lawson explained. In more than two hours on the phone, Lawson spoke freely about the events that have made him the chief target for non-Calvinists who fear that Reformed theology will split the SBC. Lawson spoke with complete confidence that he had done the right thing at Dauphin Way. According to press reports when he resigned in 2003, attendance at Dauphin Way declined from more than fifteen hundred in 1996 to about six hundred and fifty. Church membership dropped from seven thousand to three thousand, though Lawson says these figures are exaggerated. Either way, the conflict was dramatic.

"I refer to it as the Civil War, World War I, World War II, the Korean War, Vietnam, and Gulf War I," Lawson told me about his fights with the church. "It was Gulf War II that got me."

Gulf War II for Lawson was Calvinism. But it says much about today's denominational politics that so many believe Calvinism split Dauphin Way. Other factors probably played a larger role. In one instance, Lawson told me, a woman who had donated one million dollars for the church building asked Lawson to remarry her after her husband died. Lawson refused because her fiancée belonged to the Church of Christ, which Lawson said teaches a false gospel of regeneration by baptism.

In another case Lawson learned that two choir members lived together. He proceeded with church discipline and confronted them. They didn't appreciate his inquiry. So he returned with a couple of witnesses. When that attempt failed, he approached their Sunday school department. But their friends in the church backed them against Lawson. Undaunted, the next time the church took Communion,

Lawson announced that the two choir members would not be invited to partake.

Lawson finally surrendered in 2003. Two days before Christmas 2002, Lawson said, every church member received an anonymous letter in the mail. A card inside asked, "Are you a Baptist or are you a Calvinist?" The letter invited members to check the appropriate box and remit the card. The group behind the letter sent a copy to local media. That's when Lawson knew he could not continue. The entire church staff left with him, along with forty-one of forty-eight deacons.

"Steve had no reason to resign," said Rick Melson, then minister of music and worship. "He really shouldn't have resigned. He was faithfully leading that church."

The remnant who supported Lawson formed the core of his new church, Christ Fellowship Baptist Church in Mobile. He did not plan to start a church, especially not in Mobile. But the members who left Dauphin Way with him asked Lawson to give one last sermon. They rented a warehouse, and four hundred people showed up that first Sunday. In his new church, Lawson preaches the doctrines of grace without reservation.

Lawson told me he never used the word *Calvinism* in eight years at Dauphin Way. "I simply tried to use biblical language drawn from the biblical text to establish these truths," he said. "In many ways, this made for even stronger preaching because it used the language of God's Word itself."

Yet Dauphin Way responded ferociously when he preached through John 17 (particularly verse 6: "I have manifested your name to the people whom you gave me out of the world. Yours they were, and you gave them to me, and they have kept your word."). Before he preached on Romans 8:29 ("For those whom he foreknew he also predestined to be conformed to the image of his Son, in order that he might be the firstborn among many brothers"), the chairman of the deacon board—one of the most powerful men in town—warned Lawson not to continue. The chairman said the sermon would divide the church. "Better to be divided by truth than united in error," Lawson responded. He never saw the deacon again.

Lawson can cite chapter and verse with the best and exudes confidence in his ability to understand and explain the Word. Not surprisingly, Lawson has found solace in pastors who have endured great tumult, including John Calvin, Charles Spurgeon, and especially Jonathan Edwards.

"All of these great men have paid a great price," he said. "Suddenly I realized that I'm in a long line of godly men. To deny these truths would be to step out of this line."

Reading press reports about Dauphin Way's split, Lawson does indeed sound like Edwards. One pastor who stepped in after Lawson resigned said the church would have given him more support "if he had a more compassionate spirit and related more to people. He was distant . . . from everything in the church except preaching."

I asked Lawson if he would have acted differently in retrospect. Without hesitation he said no. "I don't mean to say I'm perfect," Lawson said. "By that I mean that I believe in the sovereign providence of God. God ordered my steps to come to Dauphin Way. God brought me to that church to preach his Word as an expression of his mercy and grace."

But he definitely doesn't recommend that other Reformed pastors should accept calls to lead Southern Baptist churches that do not share their Calvinist convictions. The Church of England ejected the Puritans, Lawson reminded me. Luther couldn't reform the Roman Catholic Church. Mohler may have turned around Southern, but he could fire faculty, so long as the trustees supported him. A pastor has the authority to hire his secretary and janitor.

"You only have one life to live," Lawson says to young pastors. "Do you want to drive a car that when you push on the gas pedal, someone else steps on the brake?"

Retired Southern Baptist pastor and convention president Jerry Vines did not mention Dauphin Way by name in October 2006 while preaching at a Georgia church, warning against the danger of Calvinism. He didn't need to. Vines offered his own reasons for the resurgence. He cited a reaction to the "weak commitment of seeker-friendly theology" on the one hand and dead churches on the other.

He also attributed the resurgence to conferences with popular and articulate Calvinist spokesmen.

Vines stoked his audience with a story about one good Baptist youth who grew up in Vines's Jacksonville church and attended a non-SBC college. There he embraced Reformed theology and later earned a PhD. For a time this man taught at an SBC seminary. But eventually the subject of Vines's parable left the SBC altogether for a Reformed seminary. To the audience's horror, Vines said that this man now baptizes infants.

In June 2007 every SBC church in Florida received a free DVD of Vines's message. Vines assured me that no money collected from the state's churches had been used to pay for postage. But he said that even if those funds had been tapped, that would be no different from his money funding Calvinist professors at SBC seminaries. The resurgence of Calvinism in the SBC deserves a spirited response, Vines told me that month.

"I have preached for John MacArthur. I preach up at Southern Seminary. I delivered Mohler's lectures on preaching this March and had great fellowship there. I've had Calvinists through the years preach for me. It's never been a problem," Vines said. "We're having a problem today because there's a small group of hostile, aggressive, militant Calvinists. They kill evangelism, and they kill churches. And they do it without integrity when they come in under the radar and the people don't know up front where they are theologically."

Does this militant group include Founders Ministries? "Yes," Vines responded.

If Vines is correct, can anything forestall more church splits or even a convention split? Bill Harrell, chairman of the SBC executive committee, likewise faulted some Calvinists for undermining SBC churches.

"If a man wants to answer a call to a Calvinistic church he should have the freedom to do that," Harrell told *The Christian Index* in 2006, "but that man should not answer a call to a church that is not Calvinistic, neglect to tell them his leanings, and then surreptitiously lead them to become a Calvinistic church."[3]

---

[3]J. Gerald Harris, "Martinez Pastor on National Stage Representing Georgia Baptists," *The Christian Index*, October 26, 2006; http://www.christianindex.org/2715.article.

I asked leading SBC Calvinists—including Tom Ascol from Founders Ministries—about these charges. No one condoned dishonesty. Certainly no one confessed a desire to thwart evangelism or derail churches. But many asked how they could be expected to explain Calvinism to congregations that don't understand the term. Many Southern Baptists who think they do understand probably conflate Calvinism with hyper-Calvinism, as do some leading SBC academics and pastors.

"They have put us in a no-win position," Ascol said. "If we go in with cards on the table and say we're five-point Calvinists, then we get accused of pushing our Calvinism. But if we go in and say we want to teach the Bible and we're confessional, they say we're deceitful because we didn't mention Calvinism."

Tom Schreiner teaches New Testament at Southern and preaches at Clifton Baptist Church in Louisville. What would he do? "If a church asked me, 'Are you a Calvinist?' I'd say, 'Yes, but I don't use the word *Calvinism*. I teach what Scripture says, and I explain it in terms of biblical theology, what the Bible as a whole is teaching, the framework of Scripture. That's what I want to teach this congregation. I want this church not to be a Calvinistic church but a biblical church. Now I think there's a lot of overlap there biblically. But we're not indebted to John Calvin; we're indebted to the Scriptures at the end of the day.'"

"It is simple in the sense that you go into a church and you teach the Scriptures and you love the people," Schreiner said. "That sounds easy, but it's hard. You have to be patient. You can't expect to turn things around quickly. It doesn't always succeed. Maybe the church is so immature that they kick you out. Maybe you're so immature that you get kicked out."

Debates about Calvinism in the SBC have much to do with the convention's original purpose. The SBC organized in 1845 to facilitate evangelism and missions. Some non-Calvinists fear that if Baptists believe God predestines the elect, they will lose their motivation to share their faith.

"If one does follow the logic of Calvinism, then a missionary or evangelistic spirit is unnecessary," SBC president Frank Page wrote in his 2000 book, *Trouble with the TULIP*.

This fear dogs Calvinists despite their track record of zealous evangelists, including George Whitefield, Charles Spurgeon, William Carey, and Adoniram Judson. Spurgeon and Carey, at least, did face opposition from hyper-Calvinists, who say Christians should not presume upon God's sovereignty by offering the gospel to anyone who would hear. I asked Page about his comment about Calvinism and evangelistic spirit. Would he change anything if he wrote the book today? He would be less strident about some comments, Page assured me, including the sentence I quoted.

"That's a good place where I should have pointed out that I was referring there to the hyper and/or extreme forms of Calvinism, which in many cases does dull one's evangelistic passion," Page said. "Most of the lack of passion for evangelism in the SBC comes from non-Calvinist churches."

Page can't claim the SBC's most provocative comments about Calvinism. Those might belong to Steve Lemke, provost of New Orleans Baptist Theological Seminary. "I believe that [Calvinism] is potentially the most explosive and divisive issue facing us in the near future," he warned in 2005. "It has already been an issue that has split literally dozens of churches, and it holds the potential to split the entire convention."

Lemke sees the rising generation of Southern Baptist ministers as "the most Calvinist we have had in several generations." He doubts that Calvinism has yet reached its high-water mark in the SBC. And that spells trouble, according to Lemke. Baptism and membership figures, he said, show that Founders churches lack commitment to evangelism.

"For many people, if they're convinced that God has already elected those who will be elect . . . I don't see how humanly speaking that can't temper your passion, because you know you're not that crucial to the process," Lemke explained. He told me that growing up, he learned that Christians have blood on their hands if they do not share their faith. That personal responsibility for the eternal destiny of friends and family should drive Christians to evangelize, Lemke told me. By itself, love for God doesn't suffice as motivation.

Fisher Humphreys, a former Lemke colleague, has the kind of southern name that begs for a drawl. He taught at New Orleans Baptist Theological Seminary before moving to Beeson Divinity School in Birmingham, Alabama. His books have been sent to pastors throughout the South as resources they can use to oppose Calvinism. He graciously invited me to his townhouse, where we talked through tough issues with the formality and collegiality only possible in the South. His gentlemanly tone made it possible for us to enjoy a conversation that could have otherwise become quite tense.

"Southern Baptists are very committed to this motivation: If we tell them, they can be saved. And if we don't, they can't," Humphreys said. He argued that the move away from Calvinism during the twentieth century coincided with missionary expansion. The more Christians evangelize, the less Calvinist they become, he said.

"If God did predestine, the problem you face is the universal love of God for all people," he said. "If there's anything that I believe more deeply than everything else, it is that the one true God—Father, Son, and Holy Spirit—loves every person on this planet, and that means he wants the best for them and would never predestine that some of them be damned.

"If I became convinced of predestination, then I would be a universalist, because I'm so utterly convinced that there's nobody on this planet God doesn't love and want the best for," he continued. "So if I became convinced that people are saved by God predestining them, then he would predestine everybody."

Humphreys directed me toward one of his books. In it he says that the Bible contains two sets of verses, some emphasizing God's sovereignty and others focusing on God's love. For Humphreys, every other Bible verse must submit to his interpretation of John 3:16. "I'm so persuaded that God loves everybody that I can't take Romans 9 at face value where God says, 'Esau have I hated,'" Humphreys said.

Isn't this an inadequate way to study the Bible? The false dichotomy produces a predetermined result. Who would choose a theological system over John 3:16? Would any Baptist choose predestination over "for God so loved the world"? Of course, they don't need to make that choice. The Bible doesn't let us off the hook that easily. John 3:16 must stand beside John 3:27—"A person cannot receive even one thing unless it is given him from heaven."

Humanly speaking, God's sovereignty seems to threaten human responsibility. But Scripture affirms both truths. Even when we don't understand, we can thank God that he does not limit himself according to our understanding. God gives Christians all the motivation they need to share their faith. We evangelize for God and his glory, out of love for our neighbors. We have confidence because there is no greater evangelist than the Holy Spirit.

"Reformed theology rightly understood is empowering. It is anything but pacifying," said Bruce Ware, theology professor at Southern Seminary. "This is the great fear in the SBC among the non-Calvinist majority, that this theology will squelch missions. The fact is, Southern Seminary is sending more graduates to the International Mission Board than any other seminary."

I'm not sure if Bradley Cochran has plans to serve overseas as a missionary. But the Southern Seminary student definitely has a passion for the gospel. As we talked in Louisville, Bradley confirmed for me that when God changes the inside, he often leaves the outside as is. He spoke thoughtfully about the appeal of Calvinism. He handed me a list of the leading Reformed influences for young pastors. We reflected on how the doctrines of grace actually embolden evangelism.

To be honest, I felt somewhat disoriented in our conversation. Bradley, twenty-five, did not speak with the smooth, refined drawl of Louisville's educated aristocracy. His unmistakable sharp twang hinted at a rural southern upbringing. With his shaved head and facial hair, he looked less like the clean-cut graduate students I had met and more like someone who struggled to graduate from high school.

What I saw was exactly what Bradley had been. He grew up attending a mainline church with his family in rural Kentucky. But he considered Sundays to be the worst day of the week. Following his older brother's lead, he quit going to church, passing time with other activities instead. By age fifteen he had racked up a police rap sheet and developed a drug problem. By age twenty he suffered severe depression.

In God's providence, these troubles softened Cochran's heart to the gospel. His fiancée's sister led a Bible study for youths caught up in tough lifestyles. There he became worried about the state of his soul. For two months he wavered back and forth about the gospel. Finally, after drugs killed a friend, "God granted me open eyes to see the severity of my sins," Bradley said. Immediately he cast away the signs of his previous life—he ripped down his posters, tossed out his music, threw away his marijuana, poured out his booze, and called off his engagement. He also got the heck out of his small Kentucky town. Eager for a Christian environment, he enrolled at Liberty University.

He learned about predestination when a classmate loaned him some R. C. Sproul lectures and books. You wouldn't expect a Liberty student to sympathize with Calvinism. In April 2007 Liberty founder Jerry Falwell called limited atonement a heresy. Ergun Caner, president of Liberty Theological Seminary, decried the "Calvinist Jihad" in 2006 and said Calvinists are worse than Muslims. Indeed, Bradley did not at first consider predestination to be just. But the second time he read the Sproul material, things clicked, Brad told me, snapping his fingers.

"Once I bought into the doctrine of predestination, the rest of [Calvinism] was there in seed form," he said. "I had already submitted to the idea that God could do whatever he wanted with our souls and be just."

Before Bradley even understood the rest of Calvinism, fellow students began criticizing him. Those challenges only intensified his study of Reformed theology. Cochran bolstered his arguments by boasting that he had never even read Calvin. He confessed to me that he didn't handle the debates with utmost maturity, though he did persuade many to agree with him.

"I felt like Calvinism was more than abstract points of theology," Bradley said. "I felt you would get a much bigger view of God if you accepted these things, an understanding of justice and grace that would so deepen your affections for God, that would make you so much more grateful for his grace."

Even when Bradley could not explain his beliefs, he lived them. As with SBC debates, Bradley's critics argued that Calvinists lack motivation to share their faith since they believe God has predestined some to eternal life.

"I got an evangelism award at Liberty, so no one could say that about me," he said. "My passion for evangelism only intensified with Calvinism."

Almost every Reformed pastor I interviewed bragged about how much money his church gives to missions. That's one thing they will gladly boast about, because they can recognize their church members for generosity.

"There's not a Baptist church in Jackson that gives as much money to missions as First Pres. And there are Baptist churches a lot bigger than we are," said Ligon Duncan, senior minister of First Presbyterian Church in Jackson, Mississippi. "So I think in the Presbyterian Church in America there has been from the beginning a desire from our founding fathers to be Reformed and to show the world that we do not worry in the back of our minds at night about the free offer of the gospel."

The written record alone should silence critics who blame Calvinism for missionary failures.[4] John Piper calls *Let the Nations Be Glad!* "the biggest surprise I've ever written." Hardly any missions course or training program can neglect this modern classic, in which Piper famously declares, "Missions is not the ultimate goal of the church. Worship is. Missions exists because worship doesn't."[5] J. I. Packer's *Evangelism and the Sovereignty of God*, written in 1961, has helped thousands of Christians understand the relationship between divine sovereignty and human responsibility. Tullian Tchividjian, a PCA pastor in Florida, counts as a prized possession a well-worn, first-edition copy of the book, which he plucked off his grandfather's shelf. Tullian likes to think about how the book might have affected the ministry of his grandfather, Billy Graham.

In the book Packer warns his fellow Reformed believers, "We should not be held back by the thought that if they are not elect, they

---

[4]Consider also Will Metzger, *Tell the Truth: The Whole Gospel to the Whole Person by Whole People*, revised and expanded edition (Downers Grove, IL: InterVarsity Press, 2002).
[5]John Piper, *Let the Nations Be Glad! The Supremacy of God in Missions*, second edition (Grand Rapids, MI: Baker Books, 2003), 17.

will not believe us, and our efforts to convert them will fail. That is true; but it is none of our business, and should make no difference to our action."[6]

Packer certainly does not see why trust in God's sovereignty should stifle evangelism. "Were it not for the sovereign grace of God, evangelism would be the most futile and useless enterprise that the world has ever seen, and there would be no more complete waste of time under the sun than to preach the Christian gospel."[7]

Packer makes a compelling appeal to experience in order to prove that Christians trust in God's sovereignty in salvation. In their prayers Christians thank God for leading them to faith, and they ask God to lead their unbelieving friends and family to faith. "You have never for one moment supposed that the decisive contribution to your salvation was yours and not God's."[8]

No one wants to worry about evangelism and God's sovereignty when they see their churches growing. But what happens when no one responds to the gospel call? At this point Calvinists and Arminians may disagree. Packer offers four guidelines: (1) No one can orchestrate revival. (2) It's not surprising when depraved men and women reject the gospel. (3) Jesus commands us to be faithful and does not promise success. (4) God is our only hope. This truth should not make us complacent. That's not how the apostle Paul responded. "He knew that wherever the word of the gospel went, God would raise the dead. He knew that the word would prove a savor of life to some of those who heard it. This knowledge made him confident, tireless, and expectant in his evangelism."[9] Likewise, Christians should be bold yet patient, praying continually. "God will make us pray before he blesses our labors in order that we may constantly learn afresh that we depend on God for everything."[10]

The argument that Calvinists do not evangelize fails under slight scrutiny. But Calvinists tend not to see all types of evangelistic meth-

---

[6]J. I. Packer, *Evangelism and the Sovereignty of God,* second edition (Downers Grove, IL: InterVarsity Press, 1991), 99.
[7]Ibid., 106.
[8]Ibid., 13.
[9]Ibid., 116.
[10]Ibid., 122.

ods as equal. To this end, Packer writes, "If we regarded it as our job, not simply to present Christ, but actually to produce converts—to evangelize, not only faithfully, but also successfully—our approach to evangelism would become pragmatic and calculating."[11] Packer might as well directly implicate Charles Finney, the famed evangelist of the Second Great Awakening who promised that revival would surely follow if church leaders implemented his "new measures."

Charles Spurgeon worried, as did Princeton theologian Charles Hodge, about one method popular during the Second Great Awakening and still popular today, especially among Southern Baptists—the altar call. They argued that this method can create an artificial crisis. Instead of thinking about the gospel, some become preoccupied by the decision to walk forward. Later they might be tempted to place faith in the event of the altar call rather than in the God who rescued them and promises to sustain them. After he finished preaching, Spurgeon's congregants left the building in silence. Members stayed behind to speak with those who had questions.

To be sure, the sovereign God can use any means to reach his elect. I'm thankful he does. God saved me through a ministry that in retrospect did nearly everything wrong. Leaders set teenagers on edge by depriving them of adequate sleep. Student speakers shared less about the gospel than they did about their heart-wrenching experiences of losing friends and enduring sin's consequences. Some leaders deceived new students so that later during the retreat weekend they could win over the students with surprises.

By some standards the ministry worked. Scores of teenagers emotionally professed faith in Christ, but few endured for even a short while once the retreat finished. Their old friends waited back home. Churches couldn't match the retreat's emotional highs. Yet this is how God decided to reveal himself to me.

Packer foresaw these squabbles over technique because he saw them in history. One group complains so much about methods that it becomes tempted not to evangelize at all. Another group can't figure out why converts struggle with discipleship. Packer cautions, "Satan, of course, will do anything to hold up evangelism and divide Christians;

---

[11]Ibid., 27.

so he tempts the first group to become inhibited and cynical about all current evangelistic endeavors, and the second group to lose its head and become panicky and alarmist, and both to grow self-righteous and bitter and conceited as they criticize each other."[12]

Now is no time for Calvinism to make evangelicals self-righteous and bitter toward each other. Not with so great a harvest awaiting God's people around the world. Theological debates can only do so much. Calvinists, for their part, can make the critics look silly by beating them at their own game.

"We're going to see a lot more emphasis on church planting," Tom Ascol said. "God is using the climate in the Convention and hostility against Calvinism to send a lot of our choice young men overseas. The International Mission Board is flooded with Calvinists. It's great."

---

[12]Ibid., 95.

CHAPTER FIVE

Drug-Induced Calvinism

COVENANT LIFE CHURCH
GAITHERSBURG, MARYLAND

Centuries ago the Spanish conquest transformed religious practice in Bolivia. Roman Catholic priests accompanied the treasure-hunting conquistadores and baptized the vanquished masses. But lately Roman Catholicism, often practiced in Latin America with native spiritual rituals, is losing its grip. Thousands flock daily to Pentecostalism, drawn to dynamic full-body worship and in many cases promises of health and wealth. How can ancient liturgy compete with miraculous healing?

Thanks to these trends, the small bands of U.S. evangelicals who have invaded Latin America in recent decades on short-term mission trips have found the natives more welcoming. Still, the trips must be handled with great care if the Americans want to avoid the mistakes of earlier colonists. It's amazing what a little humility can accomplish. It can even turn a Pentecostal on to Reformed theology. Now that's a miracle. After all, Calvinism presents a God big enough to heal and reward but who also withholds his blessing and tests our faith. Nevertheless, the next time you visit Bolivia, stop by Iglesia en La Paz, a church where members experiment with an unusual concoction of charismatic Calvinism. Pentecostals there treasure TULIP as much as the gifts of the Holy Spirit, including prophecy and tongues. I heard all about this church from José Troche, whom I met in Gaithersburg, Maryland, at Covenant Life Church, the epicenter of this novel phenomenon.

José and I sat down near the offices of C. J. Mahaney, who founded the sprawling suburban church in 1977 and pastored it until 2004. He still works out of the building as president of Sovereign Grace Ministries, a family of seventy-plus churches that includes Iglesia en La Paz.

José, thirty-three, didn't volunteer much information about his former church in Bolivia. I didn't learn until the interview finished that he is pursuing his PhD in computer science from the University of Maryland. I suspect the group setting for our interview intimidated José, whose non-native English tempered evident passion. Through persistent questioning, I learned that José's aunts and uncles left the Roman Catholic Church for Pentecostalism. Those relatives brought José and his sisters to church, and José attended until he became a teenager. At that point he began to lose interest in Christianity. He excelled in school but began to despise his family's faith.

"I considered that Christianity was good for weak minds," José told me, "for people who needed to believe in something and depend on some superior being in order to deal with their lack of intelligence and capacity to live autonomously."

Though José looked down on Christians, he had to admire the sneaky way they convinced him to return to the church. In the summer of 1997, some students from Rio Grande Bible Institute in Texas visited the church to serve. They didn't know how to get to the church, so they asked José to show them the way. Then they asked him to take them to the church. Then they asked him to stay and give them a ride home. Wouldn't you know, José was attending church again.

Three months later, during the farewell service for the students, they invited forward anyone who wanted to offer his or her life to serve Jesus. José didn't fully understand what he was doing, but he walked the aisle. After the students returned to Texas, José willingly and joyfully participated in the church with no extra prodding.

Still, the next year brought struggles and confusion. He attended church regularly, but José wanted a change. So in 1998 he joined his sister and a friend and headed north to Texas for the Rio Grande Bible Institute. Over the next year, José began to understand Scripture and enjoy a close relationship with God. He even learned about something called "the doctrines of grace." Fellow students told him about the tension between human responsibility and God's sovereignty, but they stressed God's sovereignty. José didn't like the implications. Yet somehow, during the summer break, José began to agree with Reformed theology. When he returned to Iglesia en La Paz and began talking about theology, few shared his passion. In fact, opposition to Calvinism led him to step away from teaching.

Gradually the church's attitude began to change, but not because of José. In the early 1990s a youth leader from a Sovereign Grace church in Virginia beat the bushes in Bolivia looking for a church that would host a short-term evangelism team. Iglesia en La Paz accepted the offer. The trip must have been a success because it started a relationship that culminated in 2001 when Sovereign Grace Ministries adopted the church.

With the new affiliation came new responsibilities. Sovereign Grace required José's pastor to study theology. Because Sovereign Grace believes strongly in the centrality of the local church, the network's ministers train within churches. So in 2002 José joined his pastor to attend the Pastors College at Covenant Life Church in Maryland. Future pastors, at least twenty when I visited, study a rigorous theological curriculum, as in any seminary. Noted instructors, including Wayne Grudem and Jerry Bridges, sometimes visit for a week to lecture the group. The trainees immediately apply their studies to practical ministry experience within Covenant Life Church.

As José did in Texas, the pastor of Iglesia en La Paz struggled to digest the Reformed theology taught by Sovereign Grace. Any systematic theology, let alone Calvinism, can grate against free-spirited Latin American Pentecostals. But with his Bible in hand and José by his side, the pastor began to understand.

As with José, the church showed little sympathy for these new beliefs when their pastor returned and taught them. But then another pastor attended the Pastors College.

"Now the whole church is changing," José said. The adjustment progresses slowly because they lack theological resources in their language. But now the congregation has a Spanish edition of Wayne Grudem's *Bible Doctrine*. They're currently reading through some John Piper classics.

The story might read like theological imperialism. The eggheaded Americans taught the Spirit-hungry Bolivians some systematic theology. Actually, the power of Sovereign Grace's beliefs only became apparent in weakness. Church members of Iglesia en La Paz learned about Calvinism when they saw how the doctrines of grace inspired Sovereign Grace's leaders to treat them with, well, grace.

"My pastors, learning from their humble presentations of how to lead to glorify God, were more and more attracted to the practicalities of their doctrine," José told me. He lamented that some Reformed advocates lead with such strong assurance of their right thinking that they chase away people who disagree.

"When you live humbly," José said, "that makes much more of an impact on people."

C. J. Mahaney gave me the most difficult interview of my career thus far. I have endured hostile subjects, awful conditions, and ill-informed answers. But I could not prepare for how Mahaney treated me. He wouldn't stop asking me questions. He seemed to genuinely care about getting to know me. We talked about rural South Dakota. We talked about nine-man high-school football. We talked about my wife, Lauren. Mostly we laughed together and enjoyed each other's company. Mahaney has that effect on most people he meets. The only physical feature that stands out more than his shiny, bald head is his wide, ever-present smile.

Finally I dragged Mahaney into discussing my one big question. How in the world do you explain this anomalous blend of charismatic practice with Calvinist soteriology (salvation theology)?

"This could be the fruit of my pre-conversion, drug-induced state," Mahaney responded, some kidding aside. To the point, he explained, "We don't see the inconsistencies."

Mahaney may not, but history sure does. Together we racked our brains in a Starbucks on Capitol Hill trying to come up with names of pastors or theologians who wouldn't mind a little glossolalia with their TULIP. I asked about Jonathan Edwards. Some crazy stuff happened during the First Great Awakening. Just read the remarkable account of how his wife, Sarah, converted. But no, he was a cessationist—he denied that New Testament miracles happen today. Mahaney offered his hero, nineteenth-century British pastor Charles Spurgeon. He seemed pretty open to the Holy Spirit's dynamic work. Nope; another cessationist.

What about Martyn Lloyd-Jones, another famous London preacher, this time from the twentieth century? He believed that the Holy Spirit works dynamically through preaching. Now we're getting a little closer.

The lack of historic precedent since the Reformation may give Mahaney pause. But he does not think Scripture leaves us guessing about tongues. Christians may speak in tongues today, he believes. The same biblical study that leads Mahaney toward Reformed conclusions guides his embrace of charismatic gifts. He takes 1 Corinthians 14 at face value. This chapter, where the apostle Paul teaches the Corinthians about orderly worship, probably came up at least five times during the three hours I spoke with Mahaney.

Holding to Paul's cautions about tongues, Covenant Life Church does not encourage members to speak in tongues during worship services. But Paul accents prophecy, which builds up the church (1 Cor. 14:1–5). During the morning I visited Covenant Life Church, two members delivered prophetic messages. In both cases the member, known to Covenant Life leaders, stepped forward to a microphone near the church auditorium's stage. Two pastors listened to the message first and discerned its worthiness according to their gifts and understanding of Scripture. Then the musicians paused between songs so the congregation could hear the message. Both messages came transparently from Scripture and could be applied generally. One young man shared his impression that sin had engulfed some people gathered for worship that morning. He exhorted them to turn to Jesus. Not the dramatic stuff you see on Trinity Broadcasting Network. It's not like he called out the lady wearing green in the third row, second seat from the aisle. Things did get a little interesting when worship leader Bob Kauflin broke into a prophetic song that came to him that morning. But he performed the song with so little fanfare and drew so many of the lyrics from Scripture that visitors to the church might not have even known he composed the song on the spot.

The growing network of charismatic Calvinists led by Mahaney is one sure sign of the Reformed resurgence. Such a combination would have been unthinkable just a few decades ago. Since then the Sovereign Grace Network has grown to include sixty-eight churches in the United

States with eight more dotted around the world. Many more unofficially affiliate with Sovereign Grace and Covenant Life Church, the movement's flagship congregation. The Sovereign Grace movement cuts a clear profile. If you attend one of its churches, you can expect to hear the pastor stress sound doctrine and progressive sanctification. He'll talk a lot about the cross. In the bulletin you'll probably read about evangelistic opportunities and church plants. Should you want to become a member, you'll learn to prioritize the work of the local church.

Mahaney, fifty-four, now devotes his time to caring for Sovereign Grace churches, Covenant Life not least among them. The church claims about thirty-eight hundred members with twenty-five pastors on staff. Walking around the campus, Covenant Life looked and sounded like a typical suburban megachurch. Children buzzed between classrooms and the gymnasium. Members lingered in the bookstore between services. Hordes of volunteers staffed a wide array of activities. Visitors attended a reception complete with an enticing food spread. Located in a diverse area, the church draws members from across the ethnic and economic spectrum. Less typical for many megachurches, Covenant Life offers hints about its theology with simple gestures, such as room names. I walked past rooms named for Spurgeon, Calvin, and Edwards.

Mahaney retains a high profile at the church, though he stepped aside as senior pastor in 2004. After all, he groomed his replacement, Joshua Harris, who moved to Maryland and lived with the Mahaney family the same year *I Kissed Dating Goodbye* hit the best-seller lists. Beyond doctrine and priorities, Mahaney continues to influence church culture in unmistakable ways. Leaders maintain an informal, self-effacing tone. Some adopt Mahaney's trademark response to "How are you?" "Doing better than I deserve," Mahaney answers.

The simple response tells a great deal about Mahaney's theology as well as his history. "I loved sin," Mahaney told me about his teenage years. "I loved to sin. I sought to influence others to participate with me in sin. I despised what little I knew of God."

He lived for drugs. "I was not casually involved in drug culture," said Mahaney, who grew up as a nominal Roman Catholic. "I partied with passion. I was a happy guy. I would be willing to compare my happiness with anyone."

He knew only a few Christians and considered them self-righteous. They wouldn't let him cheat off their tests. He mocked what he heard about Young Life events. Who would want to shave cream off balloons when he could be high on hash?

Needless to say, Mahaney did not expect to be born again. That phrase probably sounded at first like a pretty wild, drug-induced hallucination. He was smoking hash in 1972 when a friend, who had driven from Florida to Washington, D.C., shared the gospel with him. Regeneration followed in short order. Mahaney, eighteen at the time, had no idea what happened. Though he never before had the desire to read anything but the sports pages, he picked up a King James Version of the Bible and read through the night. He knew this book contained the words of eternal life. And he didn't understand a thing. Still, Mahaney would never be the same. He sobered up, and the conversion stuck.

"I had a Reformed soteriology that night, even though I'd never heard that phrase," Mahaney said. "Had you met me that night and told me, 'You responded, then God responded to your response,' I would have said, 'You're an idiot.'"

His friend returned to Ft. Lauderdale, leaving Mahaney alone without much of a clue about what Christians do. Before long he must have learned that Christians repent, because he returned to his teachers and apologized for how he had sinned against them. Christians also gather together for encouragement, and Mahaney found a group of about seventy-five college students called Take and Give (TAG). God sanctified Mahaney's gift for influencing and recruiting others. Not long after his conversion Mahaney began speaking for the group. Students from TAG formed the core of Covenant Life Church, originally called Gathering of Believers. Some of them remain church leaders today.

If Mahaney's conversion presumed a Reformed soteriology, his past presumed openness to charismatic gifts. Not long after he became a Christian, Mahaney traveled to Florida to see his friend. He attended the friend's Baptist church, where the pastor warned him not to let anyone who speaks in tongues lay hands on him. You might say the warning backfired.

"Having been freshly converted from the drug culture, not only was I not fearful of the supernatural, I would have been fascinated by it," Mahaney said. "In some way his warning only provoked curiosity. His warning wasn't going to protect me. I was a guy who sadly and to my shame had taken LSD on a daily basis like Vitamin C. Somebody speaking in tongues and laying hands on me and praying for me was not something I would be intimidated by."

Though his charismatic tendencies make Mahaney unusual for a Reformed pastor, his Reformed theology makes him even more unusual for a charismatic. The charismatic movement has largely dismissed him as a defector. Mahaney effusively distances himself from Pentecostal excesses.

"When I say charismatic and you say charismatic, and you mean Trinity Broadcasting Network, let me be clear with you—that's categorically not what I'm about."

Mahaney believes charismatics would benefit from a dash of Jonathan Edwards's discernment. In another sign of Edwards's expanding legacy, some charismatics claim that he endorsed their practices. Mahaney admits that he doesn't resonate with much of Edwards's writing. Edwards, with a philosophical bent, writes over Mahaney's head, he says. But like other charismatics, he admires Edwards's revival leadership. "Apart from what we read in Acts," Mahaney said, "Edwards has no peer."

But Mahaney worries that some charismatics selectively quote Edwards.

"Charismatics could learn from Edwards not just approval of the unusual," Mahaney said, "but doctrinal discernment as to what is a genuine, enduring work of the Spirit and not simply a temporal, superficial, emotional experience. That is what I've sought to transfer to Sovereign Grace."

And that is one key reason why the broader charismatic movement has rejected Mahaney. Calvinism remains a tough sell in charismatic communities that prioritize concerns other than doctrine. Mahaney and like-minded theologians such as Wayne Grudem and Sam Storms have had much more success at coaxing Calvinists away from their traditional cessationism. These Calvinists profess to be "charismatics wearing seat belts," to borrow Mark Driscoll's phrase.

You can be sure that John MacArthur would have nothing to do with them otherwise. The Southern California pastor's book *Charismatic Chaos* pulls no punches in denouncing charismatic excesses. More than a few people have been surprised to see MacArthur, a cessationist, participate with Mahaney at the Together for the Gospel conference. Even more shocking, he has invited Mahaney to speak at Grace Community Church and address pastors at the Shepherd's Conference. From MacArthur's perspective, desperate times call for desperate measures. They can agree to disagree about tongues and prophecy because other issues on which they agree—such as Reformed soteriology, complementary gender roles, and church discipline—demand more urgent attention. It also helps that Mahaney sports a tremendous sense of humor and penetrating humility. Mahaney gave the first talk in March 2007 after MacArthur opened his Shepherd's Conference by blasting other Calvinists for not sharing his premillennial view of the end times. Mahaney, seated in front for the talk, disagrees with MacArthur about eschatology. Those Calvinists must have been surprised to learn from MacArthur that they cannot be "self-respecting Calvinists" (MacArthur's term) without joining the premillennial cause.

"Regardless of your eschatology, I don't think anyone saw this coming!" Mahaney said of his friendship with MacArthur.

Considering domestic and international trends, it's likely that Reformed evangelicals will become more charismatic if Calvinism continues to spread. Cessationism among American evangelicals has waned outside Reformed circles just as it has within. Certainly around the globe, Christians tend to assume that the New Testament miracles continue today. Charismatics have another advantage. They tend to prioritize evangelism. Two of the most active Reformed church-planting networks—Sovereign Grace and Driscoll's Acts 29—both make room for supernatural gifts.

If those church planters look like Jason Dahlman, then charismatic Calvinism has a bright future. Jason was wrapping up his PhD in church history from Trinity Evangelical Divinity School when we talked. For the last few years Jason, thirty-three, has sifted through Puritan preaching manuals published between 1592 and 1726. This isn't just an intellectual exercise for Jason. He plans to move to Milwaukee where he will hopefully plant the first church commissioned by CrossWay Community Church, a congregation located between Chicago and Milwaukee that isn't affiliated with Sovereign Grace but shares many of its values. Soft-spoken and academically geared, Jason doesn't fit the mold of gregarious, entrepreneurial church planters. He told me that he wants to plant a church in Milwaukee because the city offers urgent opportunities for mercy ministry. Plus, the church will be close enough to CrossWay for the parent church to offer ongoing care. Pastor Mike Bullmore, a longtime Mahaney friend, has mentored Jason for years, preparing him for this opportunity. Milwaukee also fits because Jason grew up in the first suburb north of the city. The setting appears ideal.

But Jason's background would not point toward a seminary student preparing to plant a church. During his childhood, Jason's parents met with four other couples as a home church. They had declined to join either branch of a previous church split, preferring to stick to themselves.

After high school Jason moved across the state to attend college at the University of Wisconsin-LaCrosse. He struggled to find a church he could attend. Jason scoffed at paid ministers for professionalizing Christianity. He criticized churches for spending money on buildings. He regarded theology as no more than the inferior wisdom of men. No wonder most of the kids who grew up in his home church abandoned the faith altogether.

"Theologically, there wasn't any sense of being tied to any tradition. In fact, there was suspicion of anything that would smack of human theological reflection," Jason told me. "Really, they only wanted to talk about the New Testament. If somebody would bring up a theologian or confessional statement, there was inherent distrust, because they were very skeptical of the traditions of men and much more comfortable just looking at the Bible."

Through the ministry of an Evangelical Free church, Jason repented of his critical attitude toward theology and churches. He moved to Florida after college and worked for a small missions agency. His respect for the local church and convictions about theology continued to solidify. Jason devoured books by Ravi Zacharias and C. S. Lewis.

"Reading these guys I realized that theology is important, it matters," he said. "At the same time I found out they had a healthy respect for Christian tradition. That helped shift a few religious paradigms in my mind."

More paradigms shifted when he attended Zacharias conferences. The preaching of two pastors—John Piper and Alistair Begg—struck Jason as exceptionally compelling. He had never before heard such passionate preaching delivered with conviction. He began to agree with their theology, though he didn't know their doctrine had a name until he set off for Trinity to become a pastor himself. During introductory courses on systematic theology, Jason learned about Calvinism.

Trinity also connected Jason with Bullmore, who had previously worked there as a preaching professor. Bullmore led a church-planting boot camp at Trinity that Jason attended. Bullmore's passion for the local church matched Jason's changing convictions. CrossWay Community Church sounded like the kind of place where Jason could learn and serve.

Indeed, Jason has learned a great deal. He learned how CrossWay encourages members to exercise their gifts in an orderly manner for the purpose of edifying the church. He learned an appropriate balance between respect for tradition and openness to the Holy Spirit's leading. And he learned how good theology can inspire true holiness, especially humility. That's what impressed Jason about the Puritans, despite their unwarranted reputation for doctrinaire legalism. He developed deep respect for the Puritan tradition and patterned his own ministry after theirs, with one important exception.

"The guys we all read, the Puritans and all the other great, edifying Reformed theologians, implicitly or sometimes explicitly deny the efficacy of the supernatural gifts today," Jason said. "And we just have to read those passages and wink or smile. You just love these guys, you're reading John Owen, but then you get to these passages and you think, *I can't quite amen that.*"

What we need to know about the emergence of a new ecumenical Calvinism can be learned by contrasting Covenant Life Church with Mark Dever's Capitol Hill Baptist Church in Washington, D.C. The casual observer would immediately notice many differences. Ethnicity and language aside, I can hardly imagine two churches in one metropolitan area that feel so different from each other.

First, there are matters of size and shape. Capitol Hill Baptist, a Southern Baptist church, looks and feels traditional. Inside the modest brick structure, the sanctuary fits a few hundred. Covenant Life resembles other megachurches because it looks like anything but a church. Next, an observer would contrast musical preferences. You'd be correct if you guessed the music based solely on the look of each building. Capitol Hill Baptist looks traditional and even smells traditional, and *traditional* aptly describes the music as well. At Covenant Life, some Baptists might begin discerning the nefarious work of Satan in all the raised hands that accompany contemporary music. Finally, Capitol Hill Baptist's preferred clothing style resembles the buttoned-down professionals who pull down major bucks and work long hours in the nation's capital, or at least those frantic overachievers who make little money working long hours on congressional staffs. The Covenant Life crowd dresses like those Capitol Hill power brokers unwinding on a summer Saturday. If the pastor doesn't dress up, you shouldn't bother either.

Nor do Mahaney and Dever themselves seem to have much in common. Covenant Life emerged from the Jesus Movement with a pastor who left a life of drug abuse. Capitol Hill Baptist emerged from a dying Southern Baptist congregation with a pastor who earned a PhD at Cambridge while studying the Puritans. From a young age Dever began reading through the *Encyclopedia Britannica*. In Mahaney's office you'll see the *Encyclopedia Idiotica* (surrounded by shelf after shelf of books he has read).

Yet for all that the churches obviously do not have in common, they cooperate on far more. Their shared priorities illustrate the strength of the evangelical movement overall, and of the Calvinist resurgence in particular. Both churches draw on the Puritan tradition for guidance and inspiration. They highly esteem the local church, elevating issues such as church membership and discipline. Each church makes a priority of evangelism, among the congregation and from the pulpit.

During recent years, many growing churches across North America—from Covenant Life in suburban Maryland to Mark Driscoll's

Mars Hill in urban Seattle—have acted like long-lost friends though they only recently met.

"What makes it feel like a divine work is how independent these outcroppings are," John Piper told me about the spread of Calvinism. "A few years ago Mark Driscoll and C. J. Mahaney had never heard of each other. That surprised me because they're a lot alike. They're both kind of crazy in their own way. The worship at Sovereign Grace churches is very bouncy. They jump up and down. And the worship at Driscoll's church is the loudest music I've ever heard in my life—the loudest drummer at least. And here they are holding the same theology, both given to radical church planting, and they never even knew the other existed."

If this Calvinist resurgence endures, future observers might look back and see a critical event in April 2006, the inaugural Together for the Gospel conference. Good friends Dever, Mahaney, Ligon Duncan, and Al Mohler invited three of their heroes—Piper, John MacArthur, and R. C. Sproul—to join them in addressing a crowd of about three thousand pastors in Louisville, Kentucky. Through a denomination or ministry, each man has wielded influence among evangelicals. All had become staples on the conference circuit before Together for the Gospel.

"It's not hard to hear these speakers," Dever joked as he kicked off the conference. "It's almost hard *not* to hear these speakers."

The generational dynamics at work made the conference especially significant. The four middle-aged Together for the Gospel hosts watched their heroes, each older than sixty, address a crowd mostly in their twenties and thirties. The pyramid of influence illustrated the generational resurgence of Calvinism. Long-serving pastors Piper, Sproul, and MacArthur inspired the generation that includes Dever, Mohler, Mahaney, and Duncan, who have joined them in turning thousands of young evangelicals toward Calvinism.

Though together for the gospel, the conference leaders quickly made clear that they don't agree on everything. Dever admitted that wrangling over musical styles almost prevented them from playing music at all. Eventually they compromised and allowed Sovereign Grace's Bob Kauflin to play piano and lead the crowd in signing hymns. He did not perform a prophetic song. Watching the crowd during worship allowed me to figure out who belonged to which networks. Some Southern Baptists adjusted smoothly to the moderate contemporary feel. Strange looks from Presbyterians in the crowded Louisville venue didn't deter the large Sovereign Grace contingent from thrusting their hands in the air, offering verbal affirmation during the sermons, and bouncing up and down. It's a good thing Sproul sat up front and couldn't see the spectacle behind him.

Friendly banter among the speakers set the conference's tone. Introducing Dever, Mahaney had trouble cueing the screens to project a picture. "So much for name it and claim it," Sproul jokingly shouted from the first row. Mahaney responded, "Hey, I don't believe that. Get my errors right." At various points Mahaney poked fun at himself as the odd man out among accomplished scholars. "Mark, is it or is it not true that you carried a briefcase in high school?" he asked Dever, a large, distinguished man with a voice for broadcasting. The silence answered his question. To no one's surprise, it became apparent that Mohler had done the same.

Teenage study habits aside, the group does disagree on significant issues, including baptism, church polity, eschatology, and gifts of the Holy Spirit. But Together for the Gospel stuck to its mission—to connect conservative evangelicals, especially Calvinists, who share common concerns about contemporary fads. Mohler led the conference in reading through the Together for the Gospel affirmations and denials, signed by the four hosts. The document took aim at postmodern epistemology, egalitarian gender roles, and prosperity theology, among other trends. "We are concerned about the tendency of so many churches to substitute technique for truth, therapy for theology, and management for ministry," the hosts wrote.

In his address to the conference, Mohler expressed a sense of loss because theological ground won not long ago by evangelicals had been surrendered once again. But he did not simply pine for the past. The president of Southern Baptist Theological Seminary called on the pastors to subvert a culture that says, "to be a good American means to buy a lot as our obligation to keep the economy running." Afterward Dever asked Mohler, "So, should we betray America?" "We should be prepared to betray any earthly kingdom," Mohler said as cheering drowned him out.

It's a new day in Calvinism when Baptists and charismatics have become chief spokesmen. Until the last few decades, Calvinism would have connoted sixteenth- and seventeenth-century statements such as the Westminster Confession of Faith and the Heidelberg Catechism. Most evangelicals would have associated Reformed theology with Grand Rapids, Michigan, home of Calvin College and the Christian Reformed Church. Or they thought about Philadelphia, home of Westminster Theological Seminary and the Orthodox Presbyterian Church. Now the momentum has shifted to evangelicals who affirm Calvinist soteriology but not necessarily the broader Reformed tradition of covenant theology, including infant baptism.

Unlike the zeal for Calvinism expressed by converts, traditional Reformed hotbeds must sometimes fight to ward off the contempt bred by familiarity.

"I was baptized into this phenomenon in 1968 sitting in the library of Fuller Seminary when I met a psychology student from Calvin Seminary," Piper recounted. "I was just discovering Edwards and a vision for God that was knocking me over. And I was sharing it. He said, 'I'm so sick of that stuff. I had that stuff crammed down my throat in grade school in Grand Rapids, in college in Grand Rapids, in seminary in Grand Rapids. I don't know what you're so excited about.'"

The resurgence of evangelical Calvinism has reignited debates that last raged during the First and Second Great Awakenings. Many confessional Calvinists during the eighteenth century regarded George Whitefield's open-air evangelism to be vulgar. They feared that the emphasis on conversion undermined God's work through covenants. Hymn-writer Isaac Watts, for example, sympathized with the revivals but did not participate. The Second Great Awakening of the nineteenth century, with less Calvinist influence than the first, only confirmed critical Calvinists' fears about revival.

The fears live on today in places like the Orthodox Presbyterian Church. The central role of Jonathan Edwards makes matters worse for Reformed theologians who suspect that revival misleads Christians. They deny that God involves himself in human experience the way evangelicals like Edwards have claimed. It's arrogant to presume familiarity with God, they say, and to know how the Lord works in our hearts.

"They look at Jonathan Edwards as the great mistake," Dever explained. "They look back to the First Great Awakening, Jonathan Edwards's *Religious Affections*, and say that turned Christians to the subjective, which took us out of confessions of faith and baptism and the Lord's Supper and the ordinary means of grace."

Indeed, D. G. Hart argues that Edwards marked a profound departure from Calvin's understanding of conversion. So Hart, formerly dean of academic affairs and professor of church history at Westminster Theological Seminary California, distinguishes between confessionalist Calvinists and pietist Calvinists.

"At the end of the day," Hart writes in *The Legacy of Jonathan Edwards: American Religion and the Evangelical Tradition*, "it might very well be that the triumph of Edwards and experimental Calvinism has involved the elevation of the solitary soul's subjective agonies and struggles above the grand and glorious objectives of the Reformed faith."[1]

Michael Horton has observed with joy the newfound interest in Calvinism. The J. Gresham Machen professor of systematic theology and apologetics at Westminster Seminary California, Horton serves as editor-in-chief of *Modern Reformation* magazine. He also manages to host *The White Horse Inn*, a weekly radio show addressing Reformation theology. Horton observes that Christians not overly interested in theology nevertheless worry that churches have failed to make God the center of their practice and worship. The problem stems from not considering the awesome, awful holiness of God, Horton told me. "You only need a great Savior if God really is that holy," Horton said. "Otherwise what you need is a coach and a therapist and a CEO."

Horton and some colleagues temper their enthusiasm about the resurgence of Calvinism, however. That's because it's not Reformed, according to Horton. "When we hear, for instance, the term *Reformed* used to describe a broader interest in the sovereignty of God and the five

---

[1] D. G. Hart, "Jonathan Edwards and the Origins of Experimental Calvinism," in *The Legacy of Jonathan Edwards: American Religion and the Evangelical Tradition*, D. G. Hart, Sean Michael Lucas, Stephen J. Nichols, eds. (Grand Rapids, MI: Baker, 2003), 180.

points of Calvinism, we say, 'Hurrah! That's great, that's terrific! That's not Reformed. That's five-point Calvinism,'" Horton said. "*Reformed* is defined by the whole confession, and that involves covenant theology and the whole kit and caboodle."

In general, I use Calvinism to describe the five points of TULIP. According to this definition, Calvinism is an important part of Reformed theology, which more broadly emphasizes God's sovereignty and the five Reformation *solas* (by grace alone, by faith alone, by Christ alone, by Scripture alone, for God's glory alone). But there is no perfect way to define Calvinism or Reformed theology. Some do not like the term *Calvinism* because it feels beholden to John Calvin. Others like the sound of the term *Reformed theology* but may not agree wholeheartedly with the Westminster Confession of Faith. Still more simply, they abide by "the doctrines of grace," another term for TULIP's five points.

Horton worries that the problem of naming this theology leads to focusing narrowly on a particular aspect of the system, such as God's transcendence and glory. "You know how it is when you sort of get this new, grand vision of God," Horton said. "You've just read Romans 9, and you're kind of giddy with a sense of God's greatness and your smallness. But the thing that's so rich about the Heidelberg Catechism is that it doesn't dazzle us with the blinding majesty of God without leading us to the kindness and gentleness of God in Christ as the one who fully satisfied the Father's righteous requirements in our place."

Horton also worries that Calvinist cooperation has devalued baptism. Calvinists on both sides of the baptism debate love to quote the Westminster Shorter Catechism, which famously answers the question, "What is the chief end of man?" with, "Man's chief end is to glorify God, and to enjoy him forever." But the catechism says baptism should be available to church members' children. Calvinists of all stripes would happily affirm the Heidelberg Catechism's strong emphasis on reading God's Word and hearing it preached. They share the catechism's discomfort with the Roman Catholic view on sacraments. The catechism offers persuasive biblical proofs of total depravity and unconditional election. But it also regards infant baptism as a crucial sign of God's covenant with his chosen people of all ages. "Therefore, by baptism, the mark of the covenant, infants should be received into the Christian church and should be distinguished from the children of unbelievers," the catechism explains. "This was done in the Old Testament by circumcision, which was replaced in the New Testament by baptism."

Horton, who affirms infant baptism, gets along well with credobaptist Dever largely because at least they both take baptism seriously. And despite the agreement between Westminster and Heidelberg, Calvinists have not always presented a unified front. All Calvinists can agree that they don't want to return to the time when the Reformers drowned Baptists or when Puritans in Massachusetts Bay Colony booted Baptist Roger Williams down the coast, where he founded Rhode Island.

Even so, Horton worries about the natural tendency in groups like Together for the Gospel to focus on shared doctrines, which does not include mode of baptism. So is it surprising that they could begin to subtly downplay baptism?

"We can be thrilled to death that we have transcended those days when people were exiled because of their belief in baptism," Horton said. "However, it is still a larger difference than we sometimes are willing to recognize or concede in our understandable effort to express our unity in the gospel."

Piper learned this lesson the hard way. He first proposed in 2002 that Bethlehem Baptist Church should allow certain believers who had been baptized as infants to become members without being immersed as adults. Piper explained that he did not believe the doctrine of infant baptism should be elevated to the point of precluding fellowship in the church. The Evangelical Free Church in America, for example, provides for both modes of baptism.

Piper did not argue that the church should baptize infants—only that convinced paedobaptists could become members after meeting strict standards set out by the church. In 2005 only one elder out of twenty-four dissented from a proposal prepared by Piper and two other church leaders. However, after further debates and blowback from other Baptists nationwide, including Al Mohler, as many as ten elders changed their minds, and the elders withdrew the plan. Piper remains convinced that the plan would be beneficial, because he values other doctrines more preciously than baptism reserved for professed believers. Speaking later about the controversy, Piper listed the doctrines of grace, justification by faith alone, and inerrancy as beliefs that concern him more than the mode of baptism.

No such problem has sidetracked Together for the Gospel. Ligon Duncan explained to me how the leaders manage disagreement. He listed shared beliefs on soteriology and ecclesiology as common bonds they choose to prioritize.

"Our view is that doctrine matters, and it matters a lot, and that even the issues that we differ on matter a lot," said Duncan, who was the youngest-ever moderator of the Presbyterian Church in America when he served in that leadership position. "The fact of the matter is that I end up agreeing far more with Mark Dever than I do with some guys who would call themselves more consistently Reformed than Mark in certain areas because Mark has such a deeply rooted biblical view of how the life of the local church works. And so we share not only primary commitments, but we share a whole bunch of secondary commitments."

Contrary to concerns that cooperation can downplay some doctrines, Duncan says he values opportunities to explain his beliefs to evangelicals who disagree.

"We don't approach areas where we differ by saying, 'Hey, those don't really matter,'" Duncan explained. "We approach them by saying, 'Yeah, those matter a lot, and I don't want Mark's people not to hear about those things. And I don't want C.J.'s people not to hear about those things. They need to be rooted in their pastors' best understanding of the Bible according to their own confessional commitments."

Historical orientation provides a clue to understanding the main difference between Horton and his Westminster colleagues from the Calvinists who lead Together for the Gospel. Both groups draw heavily on the past to inform their present. But each group sees itself reenacting a different evangelical era. Horton does not feel so attached to or responsible for the evangelical movement. It's too diverse and unwieldy, given Horton's commitment to the confessional Reformed tradition. The Together for the Gospel group also struggles with evangelical diversity. But they want to reclaim and reform evangelicalism, as did the early post-war evangelical leaders, including Calvinist giants Carl Henry, Francis Schaeffer, and Harold John Ockenga. Though today's Calvinists remain outnumbered, their influence leavens the evangelical movement, as seen in movements such as The Gospel Coalition, led by scholar D. A. Carson and pastor Tim Keller. The growth of the Reformed ranks, especially among youth, portends significant changes ahead.

In the meantime, commitment to gospel proclamation and conversion holds Piper and company in the evangelical camp, no matter how unwieldy. Together for the gospel, they cooperate in order to advance God's kingdom. Here, too, it's instructive to learn from the past. Spurgeon, hero to Mahaney and many other modern-day Calvinists, modeled both evangelical cooperation and concern. He did not shy away from sounding the alarm in evangelicalism, as he did during the Down-Grade Controversy. Spurgeon discerned a rapid decline in theological integrity and morality in the church leaders of his day. He foresaw trends that one century later would cripple the church in Britain.

"Even if he was a cessationist," Mahaney said, "it's a gift of the Holy Spirit to look that far in advance."

But Spurgeon also modeled evangelical cooperation by appointing paedobaptists to head his Pastors' College and orphanage. Today's zealous young Calvinists would do well to heed Spurgeon's caution against allowing election to split evangelicals.

"The doctrine of election, like the great act of election itself, is intended to divide, not between Israel and Israel, but between Israel and the Egyptians—not between saint and saint, but between saints and the children of the world," Spurgeon wrote. He also stated:

> A man may be evidently of God's chosen family, and yet though elected, may not believe in the doctrine of election. I hold there are many savingly called, who do not believe in effectual calling, and that there are a great many who persevere to the end, who do not believe the doctrine of final perseverance. We do hope that that the hearts of many are a great deal better than their heads. We do not set their fallacies down to any willful opposition to the truth as it is in Jesus, but simply to an error in their judgments, which we pray God to correct. We hope that if they think us mistaken too, they will reciprocate the same Christian courtesy; and when we meet around the cross, we hope that we shall ever feel that we are one in Christ Jesus.[2]

[2]Quoted in Iain H. Murray, *Spurgeon v. Hyper-Calvinism: The Battle for Gospel Preaching* (Edinburgh: Banner of Truth, 1995), 112.

CHAPTER SIX

Forget Reinvention

NEW ATTITUDE CONFERENCE
LOUISVILLE, KENTUCKY

Walking to my seat for the opening night of the New Attitude Conference, an unexpected sound boomed over the convention center speakers. Could it be? Nah. Hip-hop? Here? With this crowd? At least the lyrics sounded about right for New Attitude, which attracted about three thousand twenty-somethings to Louisville. "Grace—unmerited favor toward those who deserve wrath," Curtis Allen rapped. "Grace is salvation from predestination. Christ gave his life to change our destination."

Curtis didn't repeat his performance during the three-day conference, but his opening rap left an impression. I approached him between sessions and asked him about a phenomenon I never anticipated writing about—Reformed rap. Curtis, thirty-three, stands at the center of a small group of hip-hop artists who employ Calvinist theology in their lyrics. A large man wearing an even larger shirt, Curtis was dressed in jean shorts that hung well below his knees. He told me all about the difficulties faced by a black man trying to reach mostly white audiences in the Sovereign Grace church network. Curtis previously worked on the staff at Covenant Life Church and still attends the Maryland church, but now he devotes his full attention to music. Curtis, who raps under the name Voice, handed me a copy of his latest album, *Crucible*.

"Man is totally depraved—see Genesis 3 and believe," Curtis raps in "If God Needs Help," a *Crucible* track. "On his own, man would never choose holiness. He's incapable, so Christ chose holes in his wrist. To demonstrate his grace to save any, though, some would argue that it's faith that saves many, apart from him, like he'll just sit back, watch, and hope some believe before their heart stops; does that sound consistent with the God of the Bible, all-powerful but in salvation he's idle?"

Voice then breaks into the refrain. "If God needs help and that's really true, does that mean salvation is up to me and you? If Christ can create the earth, moon, and stars, does his work not work unless it works for us?"

As a teenager, Curtis was about to land a record contract when police arrested him following a gang gunfight. Curtis had been dealing drugs, and police charged him with felony assault with a deadly weapon, second-degree assault, reckless endangerment, and possession of a gun. He faced forty-three years in prison. Somehow a judge sentenced him to only twenty months in jail with probation.

Curtis thanked God for the unmerited leniency. He began attending a Pentecostal church, but friends encouraged him to attend Covenant Life. Before making the move, Curtis received a copy of Wayne Grudem's *Systematic Theology* from a friend.

"I read this book and said, 'I think I've always believed this about God. I just never knew that someone had created categories for me to understand total depravity, election, progressive sanctification, everything this big blue book was telling me,'" Curtis explained. The Reformed theology gave him no trouble. "It was the gospel," he said. "I felt like it gave God the most glory."

Still, something troubled him about Covenant Life. "It was really an expression of my pride in being black," Curtis said. "I didn't want to go to a church that was predominantly white because of music preferences and stylistic things."

He stuck with Covenant Life, but Curtis stopped rapping. He wanted to leave behind this powerful symbol of his past. Then Joshua Harris, senior pastor at Covenant Life, asked him to give hip-hop another chance. Curtis first performed at New Attitude in 2006 and even released an album, though Curtis strained to make the music more accessible to white audiences.

In the fall of 2006, Curtis got a big break. John Piper invited him to perform at Bethlehem Baptist Church. Piper introduced Curtis and noted that no one had ever rapped at Bethlehem. Curtis rapped with no inhibition and received appreciative applause from the congregation. Yet when a video of the event later hit the Web, a blog firestorm erupted. One critic said of Curtis, "[H]is testimony about how God delivered him from sin and hopelessness would have been clearer without the thumping that not only surrounded his hopelessness but helps push others further into it."[1]

Critics also chided Piper for using rap music in a church worship setting, and some took the opportunity to criticize Calvinism itself. The reaction surprised and discouraged Curtis. But he refrained from responding in kind. He wrote back to one blogger and thanked him. His graciousness defused the situation. The blogger asked him for forgiveness, Curtis said. Maybe Jesus had the right idea when he told Christians to turn the other cheek.

When we talked at New Attitude, Curtis was excitedly awaiting the first album from a new record label he helped create. Every album released by Subtitles, a division of Lampmode Music, will reflect a Reformed perspective. Not that Reformed theology has suddenly become popular with consumers of Christian music. "If we were trying to please people, we would not be Reformed with our music," Curtis said. "It would be fun for the whole family."

Curtis had high praise for another Reformed rapper, Shai Linne, who joined us for the conversation at New Attitude. Shai, thirty-two, dressed casually but neatly in a button-up shirt and loose-fitting blue jeans. Curtis pointed out that this outfit would not fly in his neighborhood. But Shai attends Epiphany Fellowship, which meets near Temple University in Philadelphia.

For most of his childhood, Shai considered himself an atheist, a rare but growing group among African-Americans. Shai's mother took him to church for many years, but he preferred to argue with Christians, especially her. Suddenly and unexpectedly God changed his heart in 1999.

"From the very beginning, because of the circumstances of my conversion, I never had an issue with the sovereignty of God," Shai remembered. "I never wrestled with election, because prior to coming

---

[1]Curtis "Voice" Allen, "An Emcee's Gentle Word," *Boundless* webzine, Focus on the Family; http://www.boundless.org/2005/articles/a0001467.cfm.

to Christ I was very much anti-Christianity. When the Lord's grace snatched me up, it was the most humbling thing in the world."

Reformed theology seemed evident to Shai while reading the Bible even before he understood the terminology. So he loved Phil Ryken's preaching at the famed Tenth Presbyterian Church in Philadelphia. He so enjoyed the expositional preaching that he began listening to the sermons of late Tenth Pres pastor James Montgomery Boice. But like Curtis, Shai didn't feel totally comfortable in the church. Singing the hymns actually hurt his throat. So Shai stuck with his first love, hip-hop, and integrated Reformed lyrics. He didn't even know Calvinism stirred controversy until some began to object to his rap, such as when he placed snippets of Piper sermons in his songs. In one track called "Hell," he even referenced Jonathan Edwards's sermon "Sinners in the Hands of an Angry God."

Epiphany Fellowship, launched in September 2006, fits Shai more naturally. One pastor is a founding member of The Cross Movement, a pioneer in Christian hip-hop. Epiphany Fellowship is also part of the Acts 29 Network, a group of emerging Reformed churches led by Mark Driscoll.

Theologically speaking, Shai argues that hip-hop might be a superior musical form because of the sheer word count. "The power of hip-hop is because it's primarily a lyrical medium. It has ability to communicate large amounts of information at one time. When you're able to do that, you're able to transmit a worldview."

For a host of reasons, hip-hop has gone mainstream. Contrary to the urban grit seen in many hip-hop music videos, many rap listeners live on shaded suburban streets. Hip-hop's downside is plain for everyone to see. Many videos glorify money, sex, and violence. But hip-hop proponents point to other fundamental attractions.

"There's something about hip-hop that is similar to the rock music of the 1960s and 1970s," Shai said. "It's able to capture the hearts of the listener as the artist communicates a similar experience. So when a Tupac [Shakur] is talking about what's going on in his hood, millions of youth say, 'Yes, that's like me. I identify with that.'"

Somehow millions identify with this music even when the scenes don't reflect their experience. If they don't share common experiences, they respect the artist's raw honesty.

"Christian hip-hop uses the same form, but we're blasting a message that completely clashes with the culture at large. People latch on to that because there's an honesty and authenticity about it," Shai said.

"One of the mantras in hip-hop is 'represent.' Be proud of who you are. Stand up. Represent your clique, the group of people you hang out with. Be bold and in your face about who you are. For us, we take the same idea and say, 'Represent. Don't be ashamed of the gospel. Represent the Lord Jesus Christ.'" This idea has crossed over into the popular lexicon with the catchphrase "Keep it real."

Believe it or not, hip-hop's mainstream popularity tells us something about the resurgence of Calvinism. Like hip-hop, Calvinism taps into a universal youthful longing for community. Conversion stories reflect shared experience despite diverse circumstances. Aiding community, Calvinism's five points compose a clear rallying point. Arminianism represents such a broad spectrum that its tenets cannot similarly unite a movement.

Likewise, young Calvinists often speak about authenticity. They proudly and boldly represent their beliefs. And they talk of reading Scripture with fresh honesty when they become Calvinists. But few describe their conversion to Calvinism as a mere intellectual exercise. Many catch a passion for Calvinism when they observe and experience the difference it makes in a friend's life. They see that changing theology necessarily changes behavior. Doctrine dictates deeds.

After Curtis Allen finished at New Attitude, the guitar-driven rock music sounded more like what I expected. Over three days we repeatedly sang "Grace Unmeasured," written by Covenant Life's congregational worship leader, Bob Kauflin. With thousands of hands thrust in the air, the crowd sang, "Grace unmeasured, vast and free, that knew me from eternity, that called me out before my birth to bring you glory on this earth."

After the first set, conference founder Joshua Harris stepped forward. Though slight and short, he commands a strong, natural presence onstage. Only thirty-three, he has been speaking before large crowds for more than a decade now. His book *I Kissed Dating Goodbye* first topped Christian best-seller lists in 1998. Even before that, he wrote and spoke on behalf of homeschooled children. But this evening he introduced the purpose of New Attitude.

"Behold the truth revealed in the Word of God. Commit to believe in it. Represent it with humility," Harris told the crowd. "This is what we call humble orthodoxy. We're not showing up on the scene as a generation wanting to say, 'Hey, we've got something new, check us out.' We want to show up and say, 'We want this truth that has always been to completely transform us. We want to be humble before this truth, the Word of God. We want to humbly acknowledge that the first priority whenever we encounter the truth is to live it ourselves, and then we want to humbly proclaim this truth to our lost world.'"

This theme inspired another New Attitude tagline, "Forget reinvention," which simultaneously conveys youthful defiance and entrenched conservatism. But Harris wants more than doctrinal fidelity. He wants to see transformed lives. It's not merely that Christians are right, he said. They have been rescued. "We believe in truth," he told New Attitude. "We believe in truth so much that we want to practice it."

"In view of the fact that we were dead in our sins, the only reason we see anything ourselves is because he chose to pour out his grace in our lives. That's why there's no place for an arrogant practice of discernment," Harris said. "That's why we should be motivated to relate to others we disagree with, with courtesy, kindness, compassion, and with a desire that they would come to know the good, acceptable, and perfect will of God that we have, only by mercy."

If Christians will meet today's cultural challenge, Harris said, they must couple conviction with meekness.

"A world that doesn't believe in truth will not be impressed with us if we trumpet truth and don't show it with our lives," Harris said. "If your theology doesn't shape you, then you haven't understood it." Shouldn't this response uniquely characterize Calvinists? "We didn't see the gospel on our own," Harris reminded the audience. "God came looking for us. He found us, and he changed us."

I first met Harris at the inaugural Together for the Gospel conference. I probably should not have picked a pastors' conference as the place to schedule a private meeting. He didn't even speak at that event, and we still couldn't find a quiet spot to talk. He may not command a strong physical presence, but Harris attracted a crowd wherever we went. Gracious and unassuming, Harris took time to chat with each person who approached him, even as our interview stretched late into the night.

Though Harris now pastors a congregation of thirty-eight hundred, most still remember him as "that no-dating guy." As *I Kissed Dating Goodbye* introduced Harris to the wider evangelical audience, the book earned him at least as many detractors. He now views even the negative attention as a blessing from God because he learned the cost of taking a principled stand. Near the end of our interview, Harris praised the Together for the Gospel leaders for fighting many battles and wondered whether his generation would have the courage and humility to likewise contend for truth.

"Let's be honest," Harris said. "We ain't done nothing. So we should be quiet and learn." I pointed out that Harris has waged war against dating. He recoiled as if confronted with something he'd rather forget.

"I hope that's not on my tombstone," he said. "I hope that's not what I'm remembered for. But if there's some young man or some young woman out there who was preserved for God's glory, I'll be happy to go to the grave with that. I would prefer that there would be something else, but we don't get to write our own epitaphs. *He Opposed Dating in His Day. May He Rest in Peace.*"

Before he unleashed the great dating debate, Harris grew up as a youth leader in a seeker-sensitive church. He later joined a charismatic congregation. Neither place emphasized doctrine. Both supposed that too much theology would divide the church and sap passion for evangelism, Harris recalled. "Even just thinking doctrinally would have been foreign to me," he said. But he knew enough to know that he didn't like Calvinism.

"I remember some of the first encounters I had with Calvinists," Harris said during Mark Driscoll's Reform and Resurge Conference in 2006. "I'm sorry to say that they represented the doctrines of grace with a total lack of grace. They were spiteful, cliquish, and arrogant. I didn't even stick around to understand what they were teaching. I took one look at them and knew I didn't want any part of it."

At least he didn't until he read Piper describing God's glory and breathtaking sovereignty. A short time later, Harris moved across the country, from Oregon to Maryland, where C. J. Mahaney took Harris under his wing. Mahaney groomed Harris to take over the church he had founded and led for nearly three decades. In this process, Mahaney turned Harris on to his hero, Charles Spurgeon, the great nineteenth-century Calvinistic Baptist preacher in London. Mahaney assigned him a number of texts, such as Iain Murray's *Spurgeon vs. Hyper-Calvinism*. "I would have been reading Christian comic books if left to myself," Harris told me. Mahaney's characteristic self-deprecating humor has rubbed off on Harris. So has Mahaney's passion for sound doctrine. "Once you're exposed to [doctrine]," Harris said, "you see the richness in it for your own soul, and you're ruined for anything else."

I heard similar stories from young Christians everywhere I traveled. A vision of the transcendent God takes their breath away. When they see that theology can drive a deeper and more passionate relationship with God, they tend not to worry about potential debates over doctrine. Harris told me that a few years after he graduated from high school, he bumped into his old youth pastor in the grocery store. The pastor seemed apologetic as they reminisced about their youth group's party atmosphere, which focused more on music and skits than on Bible teaching, Harris said. But the youth pastor told Harris his students now read through Grudem's *Systematic Theology*.

"I think there's an expectation that teens can't handle that, or they'll be repulsed by that," Harris told me. "[My youth pastor] is saying the exact opposite. That's a dramatic change in philosophy in youth ministry."

The change could not have happened if young evangelicals thought Calvinism would lead to debates for the sake of debating. But Reformed spokesmen like Harris present theology as anything but dry intellectualism. It must bear fruit during everyday challenges.

"People who have never really had clear doctrinal definition in their life don't understand the importance of theology, its beauty and goodness, not just so you can debate someone else," Harris said. "True doctrine, biblical doctrine, the truth about God, is incredible comfort for the soul. It shapes the way you live."

Spending even a few minutes with Harris and Mahaney will show that they live what they preach. I'm not sure the good folks of Covenant Life Church have considered that it's not smart for the former senior pastor to retain the church's biggest office. What an ego blow for the new pastor. But that's just what I found when I visited. I can think of a number of churches where this situation would result in conflict and confusion about leadership. With Mahaney working for Sovereign Grace but still a visible presence at the church he founded, does anyone go behind Harris's back and plead with his mentor? I don't think Katherine Reynolds, Harris's assistant, ever considered this possibility before I asked her. It just doesn't happen, Katherine said. Shouldn't this humble cooperation be the norm for Christians who argue that God alone deserves all glory?

"If you really understand Reformed theology, we should all just sit around shaking our heads going, 'It's unbelievable. Why would God choose any of us?'" Harris said. "You are so amazed by grace, you're not picking a fight with anyone—you're just crying tears of amazement that should lead to a heart for lost people, that God does indeed save, when he doesn't have to save anybody."

Spoken with all the humility in the world, many Christians still recoil at this Reformed view. No matter who we are, some parts of the Bible simply rub us the wrong way. The broader culture brands Christians as intolerant for holding beliefs far less controversial than election. Consider reaction to a basic Christian belief like the exclusivity of Christ. American culture masquerades as humble under the guise of tolerance. Christians can't help but imbibe some of this poisonous atmosphere. On a host of issues, such as homosexuality, cultural pressure has grown so intense that Christians are tempted to obscure or even change their views.

"If our generation is going to have any temptation," Harris said, "it's going to be that we're so free and accommodating and humble that we never take a stand."

But Christians must stand for orthodoxy. "That might mean someone thinking that I'm being a jerk," Harris said. "I don't want to be a jerk for the sake of being a jerk and just punch somebody in the nose. But if the truth is the truth, there has to be a willingness to be humble and kind but not budge."

Though Harris is the face of New Attitude, he did not coin the phrase "humble orthodoxy." That honor belongs to Eric Simmons, who leads the Covenant Life singles ministry. That is no small task at Covenant Life because about six hundred singles attend the church. With "humble orthodoxy," Eric consciously played off *A Generous Orthodoxy*, the title of a book by leading emergent pastor Brian McLaren. One small word can make a world of difference. What's humble to Simmons doesn't look so humble to McLaren. And what's orthodox to McLaren doesn't look so orthodox to Simmons.

I'm not sure I truly understood the moral implications of Calvinism until I sat down for dinner with Eric, thirty-four. He reminded me that Calvinism has not spread primarily by selling young evangelicals a system but by inviting them to join a new way of life driven by theological convictions. Theology gives them a passion for transformation, first their own and then others'. Eric's experience and ministry etched this point into my memory. After only a few minutes, Eric made me feel like a long-lost friend. He shared about growing up as an angry child who turned to drinking and drugs after his parents divorced. When he ran into repeated trouble at school, his mother took him to Maryland to live with his grandparents. They placed him in a Christian school.

"That school took in kids evangelistically who were getting kicked out of public school," Eric said. "By God's grace, I qualified."

Eric noticed something different about these Christians when he observed the relationship his friend had with his father, a pastor. The pastor-dad loved his son as Christ loved him, and he reached out to Eric. At church Eric sat in the front row, thanks to his troublesome reputation. One morning in church when he was seventeen, Eric could almost audibly hear God tell him, "I have set before you life and death. Choose life." His inhibitions fell away like scales from his eyes. The problem child began raising his hands to worship God.

His transformation was complete but not finished. Though not Jewish, Eric had been converted in a Messianic congregation. He made quite a shift when he started attending Covenant Life, which shared his previous church's charismatic bent but not its dispensational embrace of modern-day Israel. He picked fights with anyone foolish enough to engage him.

"I had the trifecta of what you don't want in a young Christian," Eric confessed. "I was ignorant, arrogant, and I had a loud mouth."

Covenant Life's leaders patiently endured his sin and helped him understand the problem. Before long he asked them to forgive him. Under the guidance of Covenant Life members, Eric grew in a host of other ways. In eighteen years before college, Eric had read only two books, spending countless hours parked in front of the television. But after Eric was converted, God gave him a desire to read, particularly history, philosophy, and theology. Eric immediately began reading John Owen and dove straight into the systematic theology of Louis Berkhof and Wayne Grudem. Mahaney turned him on to Jonathan Edwards and further stoked his interest in the Puritans.

"He spoke so passionately about them," Eric said. "You could see it wasn't just affecting his thinking; it was affecting his living. He talked about them like a really good burger he'd just had. *You've got to try this place.*"

What Eric received from Mahaney and the Puritans, he passes on to the singles at Covenant Life. To test them, and his own motivations, Eric sometimes goes out of his way to be uncreative. He usually preaches for forty-five minutes. He figures that you need to win people with the same methods that you expect will keep them around and help them grow. Flashy messages and loud music can't compensate for the best community builder—confession.

"Really believing in the doctrine of sin creates the most authentic communities, and young people really want that," Eric said. "They need Spurgeon and Edwards and Owen because they're the ones talking about sin."

With charisma to spare, Eric could build a large ministry on personality alone. He could treat his ministry like a glorified dating service for Covenant Life singles. Instead Eric treats his job with deadly seriousness. "You're preparing these people for cancer," Eric said. "A three-point talk on whatever's hip and in right now won't sustain them. They need a sovereign God. What do I want to see in these people when they're sixty-five?

"I don't like marketing ourselves as the next generation. I want people to be desperate not to blow it. We're inheriting a tradition, and we need to ready our hands to receive the gospel. We don't want to fumble it because we need to build local churches with it. There's a sense of urgency."

Eric and the other New Attitude leaders invited four of their mentors to address their conference—John Piper, Mark Dever, C. J. Mahaney, and Al Mohler. According to Mohler, young evangelicals are ready to take the gospel handoff.

"This is a generation that wants to say something that has been said before," Mohler told me. "They see all the plastic and liquid truth claims of the ideologies bandied about in the university. It comes as great comfort to believe that one can come to own a faith that is old and eternal and that has taken shape in confessional forms that are deep and substantial and, more than that, deeply biblical."

Indeed, many evangelicals today grow up in what J. I. Packer described to me as "a kaleidoscopic world of uncertainty." Reformed spokesmen can give them certainty, Packer said, because they confidently marshal biblical proof texts. And unlike previous eras, the sudden growth of Calvinism has made Reformed theology more credible.

If you follow Packer's argument, the spread of theological and moral relativism may have laid the groundwork for the Calvinist resurgence. As cultural Christianity disappears, Christians stand out. Consider a student who enrolls in a non-Christian college. That student's faith will not likely emerge unchanged. Social and academic pressures will send the student deeper into faith or retreating into doubt. If neighbors in your dorm loathe you simply for believing Christianity is true, what would stop you from holding other unpopular views, such as predestination? If you decide to stand your ground despite the ridicule, you will need to find encouragement from Scripture and models from history. Calvinism boasts deep biblical and historical roots, along with a stirring, countercultural message about the sovereignty of God.

This hypothesis would explain why I found many of the most

vibrant Calvinist outposts on secular college campuses and in large cities. This theory also foretells a leading role for Calvinism in the evangelical future. As the rest of America polarizes, New York City pastor Tim Keller and other leading Reformed cultural analysts will be ready to help believers find their way.

Campus Crusade for Christ, the world's largest campus ministry, has adjusted its training to meet the cultural challenge. In the process Crusade has become more hospitable to Reformed theology. Close connections with Dallas Theological Seminary made dispensationalism the primary theology in Crusade's early days. Hal Lindsey, author of the apocalyptic best-seller *The Late Great Planet Earth*, regularly taught Crusade staff in the 1970s. But mission tended to really drive the Crusade engine. Any mainstream evangelical view was welcome, so long as no one rocked the boat and distracted from the mission. For years staff had been required to take theology courses during the summer. But that rule fell into neglect in the 1980s when Crusade began to assign staff to lead beach evangelism on summer projects.

The trend worried Keith Johnson, Crusade's director of theological education and development. In 2002 he proposed a plan to train thousands of Crusade staff in core theology courses. His new training program has changed Crusade culture.

"We don't attract many Bible college graduates on staff," Johnson said. "They've had no formal theological training. We're trying to help them learn how to read the Bible; we're trying to help them see how the Bible tells one story."

Staff can earn graduate credits and fulfill their Crusade requirements at partner seminaries such as Dallas, Trinity Evangelical Divinity School, Southern Baptist Theological Seminary, and Reformed Theological Seminary. Many elect the affordability of Southern or the off-campus and satellite options of RTS.

Crusade staff themselves teach many required courses. Chris Sarver, campus director at Ball State University, teaches a core summer class on biblical communication. He uses John Piper's *Seeing and Savoring Jesus Christ* as a text, along with *Christ-Centered Preaching* by Bryan Chapell, president of Covenant Seminary in St. Louis. The selection didn't surprise me. Sarver led me through Grudem's *Systematic*

Theology when he served as Crusade's campus director at Northwestern University. I thought our little Crusade ministry was pretty unique for teaching Reformed theology. But with Crusade's renewed emphasis on theological training, staff like Sarver have become more common. They model commitment to the mission but recognize the need for a solid biblical foundation.

"As the culture is shifting, there won't be a one-size-fits-all strategy," Sarver said. "So we need leaders who are creative but grounded biblically and theologically."

Crusade tends not to operate on campuses like Baptist-affiliated Samford University, deep in the Heart of Dixie in Birmingham, Alabama. Samford has too much Christian influence for Crusade to feel needed. About half of the nearly three thousand undergraduates at Samford University grew up in Baptist churches. A few hundred apiece claim Methodist and Presbyterian backgrounds. Plenty of other campus ministries have found Samford to be fruitful ground. But Baptist parents might want to avert their eyes.

"The three most successful campus ministries in Birmingham—Reformed University Fellowship, Campus Outreach, and University Christian Fellowship—are all heavily Reformed," Matt Kerlin, minister to the university at Samford, told me.

According to Kerlin, college students on their own for the first time have the right balance of curiosity and maturity to reconsider their theological upbringing. College also tends to be a time when students work through perennial topics such as God's will, suffering, and predestination. Kerlin has said that lately he can always pack the Samford chapel when he schedules a talk about Calvinism. Though by no means Reformed, Kerlin has found a silver lining in this theology's growing popularity.

"It means that instead of talking about drugs, I have lots of theological conversations with students," Kerlin said. "I would rather students stay up late talking about Calvinism than I would college football." Kerlin has also found students paying closer attention to their Bibles as they debate predestination.

Campus Outreach started at nearby Briarwood Presbyterian Church, one of the largest PCA churches in the country. RUF is the official PCA ministry. But University Christian Fellowship dwarfs them both at Samford. I didn't plan to make Birmingham a stop on my Reformed tour. But then I heard about UCF, which draws about seven hundred of its one thousand students from Samford. I met Joel Brooks, the UCF founder and director, in the ministry's brand-new, nine-hundred-thousand-dollar house on the campus of Mountain Brook Community Church. Joel told me he raised three hundred thousand dollars in just a couple weeks after sending one letter to supporters.

The house includes a full kitchen, and we had only one interruption during the interview, when a student stopped by to do her laundry. Joel spent eight thousand dollars acquiring theology texts, shelved near a comfy den complete with a fireplace. He teaches from the stage in the large open area near the front door. The area is well-suited for small concerts. UCF hosted Derek Webb and Phil Keaggy not long before I visited. Upstairs, students can use the UCF recording studio at no charge. There's only one catch. Students must be accompanied in the studio by UCF staff. That's not to make sure the equipment is safe. That's to make sure the students don't record bad music. Joel wants to uphold all three legs of the UCF motto: "Faith. Art. Community."

Joel, thirty-four, wore a simple green T-shirt, blue jeans, and tennis shoes. Like his attire, Joel spoke with an informality that barely hinted at his considerable gifts. Joel grew up immersed in the church. His father had been a Baptist deacon, and his mother played the organ. He accepted Christ when nine years old. When other kids announced their dreams of becoming firemen or astronauts, Joel said he wanted to be a pastor. So in college at the University of Georgia, Joel prepared by majoring in speech and religion. But those studies took a backseat to his real preparation, a practice he has maintained ever since. Joel wakes up every day between 4 and 4:30 A.M. and starts off with two hours of reading, one hour with the Bible and one hour with a theology text.

"If you're not learning, then you get burned out," Joel said. "If you don't get rubbed the wrong way by God, then you're not converted, and God will begin to look like you."

Joel's Baptist church in Georgia certainly wasn't Reformed. Joel said he once asked his pastor about Malachi 1:2–3, where the Lord says he loves Jacob but hates Esau. Paul references this verse in Romans 9:13. Joel said the pastor answered that God's choosing Jacob over Esau was like choosing vanilla over chocolate ice cream. The response did not placate Joel, who observed that God doesn't condemn chocolate ice cream to hell.

Joel embraced Calvinism during his freshman year at Georgia. It turns out that not even the Wesley Foundation is safe from Calvinism. He joined the Wesley Foundation because that Methodist group was much more conservative than the Baptist equivalent. But Calvinists had infiltrated the Wesleyan ranks. Joel picked fights with them at first, and they obliged with spirited debates. But one Calvinist shocked him by refusing to argue. He told Joel to spend a couple of weeks reading the Bible first. Joel took four weeks studying the relevant passages.

"He never even had to talk with me," Joel said. "It was like I saw Scripture through a different lens."

After he graduated from college, Joel headed across the border to Birmingham and enrolled at Beeson Divinity School on the Samford campus. Joel's Reformed beliefs deepened in a class he took with Beeson dean Timothy George, who required his class on John Calvin to read the great Reformer's *Institutes of the Christian Religion* and summarize every page. The workload for a two-hour class shocked even Joel.

He started UCF after graduating from Beeson in 1999. Joel had expected to head overseas with Greater Europe Mission. But the Lord had plans for him in Birmingham. He first turned his attention toward students at Birmingham-Southern College, a liberal-arts school affiliated with the United Methodist Church. But Joel said the chaplain objected to evangelical faith and prohibited Joel from meeting with students. The chaplain's move predictably backfired. Word spread from student to student that an evangelical had been barred from campus. In just one week Joel's Bible study grew from five students to between sixty and seventy, Joel said. Even today as he leads UCF, no other publicity can match word of mouth.

"I love that people hear about UCF, and they know it's large, and the first thing we do when they come in is spend fifteen minutes of total silence on our knees," Joel said. "It throws off a lot of the freshmen who come from youth groups."

Aside from the new ministry house, Joel offers nothing fancy—just prayer, worship through song, and teaching from God's Word. "I tell people we're a really boring ministry," he said. "If God is not your attraction, you'll be bored."

Boring seems to be booming. UCF has grown so large that Joel encourages students to attend Reformed University Fellowship and Campus Outreach. He doesn't seem too impressed with numbers. He knows size indicates nothing about gospel fidelity. Still, UCF could really use more staff. The ministry pays only one other full-time staffer, a recent Samford graduate who devotes her time to women.

Perhaps the most exciting UCF ministry happens not in large settings but with a handful of especially committed students. Joel leads a group that meets every Monday night for a couple hours to learn and recite the Bible's storyline. He has compiled a demanding syllabus. Each student reads up to forty-two Bible chapters every week. For the first semester, covering the Old Testament, students memorize a three-page chronological outline.

With this strategy, Joel hopes Scripture itself will become the foundation of UCF students' theology. In this way they might become Reformed before they know anything about labels. "If they knew the label, then they'd fight it," Joel said. "That's why we're not Reformed University Fellowship."

Not that Joel keeps his theology under wraps. He invited his hero in the faith, John Piper, to speak at UCF in November 2005. Piper delivered a tough message about how God uses suffering, even events like Hurricane Katrina, to grab our attention. Over dinner together, Piper gave Joel some advice he'll never forget. He encouraged Joel to aim so high in his preaching that he takes the students way beyond where they thought they could go. He also encouraged Joel to emulate a dead theologian, as Piper has done with Jonathan Edwards. Joel, who has read twenty of Piper's books and at least three hundred of his sermons, informed Piper that he was Joel's theologian of choice. Piper kindly explained that he really intended for the theologians to be dead. "In Minneapolis, you're as good as dead to me," Joel told him.

I left the UCF house a bit stunned that I had blindly stumbled onto such a fascinating ministry. UCF exemplifies much of what I discovered in my cross-country investigation of Reformed theology. Just one capable leader, armed with a potent Word and transcendent theology, can be the conduit God uses to bring revival. Community grows around a clear, challenging message. Authenticity develops when students can share struggles and find strength to endure in prayer and Scripture.

Joel, however, did not let me leave without mentioning one caution. He recalls his college experience and wishes more young Calvinists would just back off. If they believe in a God who acts, why would some Calvinists put such pressure on Christian friends to "convert"?

"The problem with Calvinists is that they go full steam into arguments with others over the sovereignty of God because they think God's glory is at stake," Joel said. "But arguing over this actually defeats the very belief that God is the one who sovereignly changes hearts and the will. By arguing, you prove you don't really believe the things you claim to believe.

"Humility," Joel said, "acknowledges that we all need sovereign grace in our lives, and this glorifies our God."

Talking with Eric Simmons and Joel Brooks, the common thread of community repeatedly appeared. If college provides a unique opportunity for intense community, then recent college graduates often experience a letdown. As Campus Crusade for Christ will attest, many of these students will abandon their faith if it's not reinforced by friends and peers.

"I've found that most twenty-somethings are lonely," said Justin Buzzard, twenties pastor at Central Peninsula Church in California's Bay Area. "After leaving the community they had during their college years, twenty-somethings can feel quite disoriented, confused over how to do life in the working world. Longing for community among this group shows up again and again."

Young Reformed evangelicals increasingly find community the same place where their cohorts find community—on blogs. "[Blogging] has shown people like me that we're not alone," Buzzard told me as we talked at the inaugural meeting of The Gospel Coalition at Trinity Evangelical Divinity School. New conferences, including The Gospel Coalition, have connected like-minded young evangelicals. Blogs keep them in touch between events. Blogs bring special encouragement to pastors like Buzzard, who does not serve with any other Calvinists on his pastoral staff. For that matter, he serves in a part of the country with few evangelical churches. "Blogs have created theological community across geographic distance," Buzzard said. "They have taken isolated movements and made for a collective resurgence."

Before the Web, you might learn about Reformed theology if that's what your pastor preached, if you found a Banner of Truth book in the local Christian store, or if a friend handed you a Charles Spurgeon sermon. Now you can go online and find endless resources new and old from history's leading Calvinists. "The Internet has done for Reformed theology what MTV did for hip-hop culture," said Matt Hall, who started blogging in 2003. "You never would have had a white kid in Iowa listening to Run DMC if MTV had not taken them from the Bronx and put them on cable TV."

Leading Reformed bloggers, particularly Tim Challies and Justin Taylor of Between Two Worlds, boast thousands of loyal readers (http://www.challies.com/ and theologica.blogspot.com/ respectively). I grabbed breakfast with Challies at the New Attitude conference, one of many he liveblogs. He estimates that his site attracts between one hundred and fifty thousand and two hundred thousand visitors per month. The key to blogging is consistency, Challies said. He has blogged every day since November 1, 2003.

"If you look at the Christian blogosphere, most of the well-known and highly regarded blogs are Reformed," Challies said. "The Reformed blogs tend to center around theology. They are more of a teaching tool than a talking tool."

In this Internet era, Challies has become something of a celebrity. In one forum he appeared on stage with Steve Lawson and D. A. Carson. He has also shared a stage with Al Mohler. But Challies might have been the guy the crowd anticipated most.

"They know they can't be Al Mohler. They can't be running a seminary when they're thirty-three and sleeping three hours a night and reading ten books a week," Challies said. "They look at me and think, *If he can do it, I can do it.* Blogging gives a voice to the amateur, the little guy."

The blog voice often adopts a personal tone, giving the reader a feeling of authentic connection to the author, even if the blogger remains anonymous. Blogs also invite response and discussion, which leads to a peculiar but powerful type of community wrapped tightly around shared affinities. If new media can make hip-hop popular in Iowa, then it's no stretch to think that blogs could transform evangelical theology.

CHAPTER SEVEN

Missional Mind-set

MARS HILL CHURCH
SEATTLE, WASHINGTON

Red wine and rich ales flowed freely during a dessert and drinks reception hosted by Mark Driscoll and his wife, Grace, at their Seattle home. True to Driscoll's reputation, no light beer could be found. The five young Driscoll children darted in between about fifty church planters, who clustered in small groups to talk shop. These men had converged on Driscoll's Mars Hill Church for an Acts 29 "boot camp." Over three days Driscoll and other network leaders shared about the challenges of starting a church, while prospective lead church planters met with Acts 29 veterans who assessed their fitness for the arduous task.

But on this night cheesecake and microbrews trumped concerns about evaluations. The crowd of mostly young, energetic pastors relished a couple of hours where they could reflect on the joys and frustrations unique to their clerical fraternity. The gathering produced some fascinating group dynamics. In one conversation I joined, three church planters from the Pacific Northwest discussed N. T. Wright's kingdom theology. The lively give-and-take concluded with frank missionary assessments of their communities. The tattooed church planter from Portland, Oregon, described an eclectic mix of indifference, hostility, and spiritual hunger. The pastor from one of Seattle's wealthiest suburbs explained how short-term missions helped his church members grow more compassionate. In the small western Washington town where the third pastor started a church, hundreds gather on Saturday evenings to watch demolition derbies. So his church sponsored a car and hosted cookouts in the pit area.

Before long, word spread that a journalist had infiltrated the church planters' ranks. Stories began to pour out. One older pastor from the Seattle area expressed his appreciation for the Reformed theology that Driscoll has imprinted on Acts 29. He had previously ministered in a church that adopted Rick Warren's Purpose Driven model. Another pastor from St. Louis told me that Driscoll saved his marriage. A couple of years ago he attended an Acts 29 event not unlike this boot camp. Driscoll called out the pastor when his wife confessed that he neglected her in favor of the church. A third church planter approached me and affirmed the spread of Calvinism among young evangelicals. As a youth pastor in a large nondenominational church in Bakersfield, California, he developed Reformed convictions. Soon the high-school students requested books from John Calvin and Jonathan Edwards—that is, until their parents found out and banned the Reformed authors. So they picked up the works of John Owen, a lesser-known Puritan. Rebellion takes many forms.

These pastors afforded me a glimpse into Driscoll's growing sphere of influence. If you grow a church of six thousand in some of the nation's most difficult spiritual terrain, other evangelicals will start asking for advice. In one week in 2006 as he prepared to teach at John Piper's Desiring God conference, Driscoll received speaking invitations from Jerry Falwell, Robert Schuller, and Bill Hybels. And yet it seems that many evangelical leaders don't like everything they hear from Driscoll, thirty-seven. His open ambition to build a large church and transform Seattle grates against many Calvinists. His willingness to accept members who drink offends Baptist teetotalers. His unflinching Calvinism scares away emergent gurus. No one can claim him. So all turn their guns on him.

Having seen Driscoll in person, I can confirm that he does not have a sloped forehead. He didn't appear to be drunk. And if he packed a firearm, I couldn't see it. For all his supposed patriarchal tendencies, Driscoll welcomed me to his home with a hearty hug. So much for stereotypes.

Actually, for as many stereotypes as Driscoll dispelled, he confirmed many more. That much became clear as we sat down for a few hours in his study, situated above the garage next-door to his beautiful new home in a pleasant Seattle neighborhood. Little he said would appease critics upset about his views of male headship or frustrated by his confrontational preaching style.

Driscoll didn't bother to walk me through his many shelves of theological treatises and Bible commentaries. But he did show off two prized possessions—a baseball bat broken by Reggie Jackson and a letter penned by Charles Spurgeon. Both men, I may observe, had larger-than-life personalities and swung for the fences, just like Driscoll. Our conversation ranged across a variety of topics, from the challenges of postmodernism to the problems with fundamentalism. We talked about the stress of leading a megachurch whose ever-growing profile has attracted the interest and ire of evangelicals far and wide. And we discussed how Reformed theology both confronts and comforts a city that tolerates anything but intolerance.

Seattle might be home to Microsoft, but it feels more like an Apple town. Independent and creative, Seattle has reared multinational corporations like Boeing, Starbucks, and Amazon.com. Yet Seattle also hosted violent protests against globalization during the 1999 World Trade Organization meetings. The city remains uncomfortable with the success that resulted when entrepreneurs thumbed their noses at convention.

In all this growth and tumult, churches have played a bit role. The evangelical movement never reached the Pacific Northwest in any significant numbers. Even today less than 10 percent of Seattle's residents identify with evangelical churches, and fewer still worship in mainline Protestant or Roman Catholic churches. Various cultural streams flow into Seattle and create an eclectic mix that any prospective missionary must understand. Seattle feels something like a cross between the Far East and northern Europe. Worldviews as diverse as Wild West individualism and Wicca form the city's spiritual attitudes.

Leaders at Mars Hill Church describe their ministry approach as missional, meaning Sunday mornings prepare members to act as missionaries within their community throughout the week. For the people of Mars Hill, so named for the apostle Paul's missionary visit to Athens recounted in Acts 17, understanding Seattle culture is vital missionary research, not to mention a mirror on their own souls.

Mars Hill's main campus meets in the Ballard neighborhood, a former Norwegian fishing village turned industrial district that is giving way to urban hipsters. Born in 1970, Driscoll grew up behind a strip club near the building where the church's West Seattle campus now meets. He graduated from high school "most likely to succeed," and it's not hard to see why. Besides serving as student body president, Driscoll captained the baseball team and edited the school newspaper. He didn't read the Bible until college when he picked up a copy given to him by Grace, a pastor's daughter who is now his wife. Driscoll first sided with the Pharisees as he read Scripture because he admired their self-control. But in the course of further reading, God revealed to Driscoll that Jesus was the hero.

After college Driscoll returned to Seattle and worked as a youth pastor. But he felt the itch to start his own church, which would combine Reformed theology with a missional strategy. In retrospect Driscoll admits that he had little clue about what he was doing when he planted Mars Hill in 1996. He didn't even bother to write out the church's nonnegotiable theological beliefs. "I also did not explain in written form that we were theologically conservative and culturally liberal, which caused great confusion because half of the church was angry that the other half was smoking, while the other half was angry that I taught from the Bible," he writes in *Confessions of a Reformission Rev.*[1]

Nevertheless, the church grew. But Mars Hill sustained heavy turnover, and Driscoll gained the reputation of a cult leader. He has never completely shaken that reputation in Seattle or even among some Christian critics.

"Some guys are by nature peacemakers and bridge builders, and some guys plant the flag in the ground and see who runs to it," Driscoll told me. "I get up and I pray and then I speak, and I don't really think about what's going to happen or how it's going to play."

He certainly could have chosen a more user-friendly theology than Calvinism. His views have firmed up with time. Preaching through Exodus early in his career, Driscoll was struck by God's sovereignty over Pharaoh. He saw how God acted to deliver his people. Preaching

---

[1]Mark Driscoll, *Confessions of a Reformission Rev.: Hard Lessons from an Emerging Missional Church* (Grand Rapids, MI.: Zondervan, 2006), 46.

through Romans eliminated any remaining doubt about Reformed theology, which he summarizes this way: "people suck and God saves us from ourselves."[2]

"I love studying books of the Bible, and I love trying to figure out in this book of the Bible how is God presented," he told me. "And that really drove me to some Reformed convictions."

Calvinist enthusiasm spread like wildfire at Mars Hill when Driscoll's views crystallized. Young men in particular debated theology for hours. But a strain of hyper-Calvinism infected some enthusiasts. They challenged Driscoll's teaching about the church's mission. He wasted no time kicking them out of the church.

This brand of leadership could hardly be considered typical for a charter member of the "emerging church" movement. "Emerging" Christians seek to follow Jesus within postmodern culture and have provoked controversy for theology and ministry innovations. For years Driscoll traveled the emerging circuit, speaking with proponents like Doug Pagitt and Tony Jones. But Driscoll should be regarded as nothing short of hostile toward key postmodern assumptions such as diffused authority. That became clear when I asked him if Scripture clearly presents his complementarian view of gender roles.

"Beyond a shadow of a doubt," Driscoll answered. "Egalitarianism is a myth invented. It's not a doctrine found. I get shot on that, and that's cool, man. I love those who disagree with me. But yep, I see the complementarian issue as a watershed issue."

Driscoll continued with other debated doctrines that he believes should be clearly understood from Scripture. "Inerrancy is a watershed issue. Penal substitutionary atonement is a watershed issue. Heaven and hell are watershed issues, and homosexuality is a watershed issue. Those are the issues for this generation."

Because Driscoll thinks Scripture allows no confusion on these points, disagreement becomes a matter of authority, not interpretation. He may speak and dress more casually than other Reformed leaders, but on this point he fits the profile.

"The root issue in a postmodern era is authority," he explained. "Is

---

[2]Ibid., 85.

there any authority? Does anybody get to say Scripture is an authority? Does a pastor get to be in authority? Does a parent get to be in authority? Does a church get to discipline anybody? Is there such a thing as a heretic? Is there anybody who gets to be a referee saying, 'That's not right'? Heaven and hell. Does God have the authority to say that some people can't be with him? Homosexuality. Does God have the right to say some people can't have sex with each other? These are all ultimately authority issues."

Of course, Driscoll would answer yes to each of these questions. He doesn't much care if you disagree. Driscoll figures tough teaching won't make Seattle any more hostile to the gospel. But he can shock the spiritually apathetic and intrigue the curious by preaching clear truth coupled with high commitment. Many respond when Driscoll explains how the gospel juxtaposes God's holiness with his grace and mercy.

"The Puritans said the same sun that melts the ice hardens the clay," Driscoll said. "When you preach hard words, some people's hearts melt and others harden. I think soft words produce hard people, and I think hard words produce soft people."

According to Driscoll, the prevailing postmodern mood means that Christians don't need to expend many hard words convincing younger generations to believe in total depravity. I pressed him on this point. Weren't the twenty-somethings in his church weaned on self-esteem?

"Yeah. And then they grew up, and they were raped and molested and abused," he responded. "They're alcoholics and drug addicts, and their parents got divorced, and they don't trust any politician, and the authority figures in their life have let them down, and their parents had free love, and now they're got STDs. . . . Everybody's jacked up."

Firsthand experience with so much pain and brokenness has deeply ingrained disillusionment in many young Americans. Cynicism reigns. Aimlessness abounds. And yet Driscoll does not dwell on how these trends threaten Christianity. With typical evangelical ingenuity, Driscoll finds the gospel opportunity in this cultural context. He has learned that youth with no church background regard traditional worship practices as foreign but intriguing. Their parents, on the other hand, might consider those same practices to be rote and meaningless. It's no coincidence that the songs played at Mars Hill include more thees and thous than the hymns accompanied by organ in many traditional churches. Driscoll encourages all Acts 29 churches to follow his lead and administer Communion each week. For similar reasons, Reformed theology does not suffer for falling out of favor with previous generations.

"There is a wandering generation that is looking for a family and a history and a home," Driscoll said. "And they're going backwards in history hoping to find a family and a home. That's true for Reformed theology, but there's also a resurgence in Catholicism, in Eastern Orthodoxy, in some of the monastic practices. There is a season right now of going back. The Reformed strain definitely is one of the most popular, but I think in part because it's one of the most written, published. It has a lot of material available."

Tony Jones has not sat down and spoken with Driscoll in five years. But that doesn't mean the coordinator of Emergent Village has nothing to say about Driscoll, who split with the group in 2001. Emergent Village was once part of Leadership Network, which whisked Driscoll around the country for speaking engagements starting in 1995.

I wanted to hear from Jones because he has tracked Driscoll over the years and takes an entirely different approach to the challenge of postmodernism. Jones attends Solomon's Porch in Minneapolis, led by longtime Driscoll foil Doug Pagitt. Both Mars Hill and Solomon's Porch could be regarded as leading outposts of the emerging church. Their differences illustrate the absurdity of lumping all emerging churches together. These congregations share little more in common than the surrounding culture.

Jones scoffs at churches that respond to postmodernism without rethinking theology. But he can see why Mars Hill has experienced such rapid growth.

"You have all these people in the shifting sands of moral relativism in Seattle, a peripatetic young adult crowd, and here's this guy who's just cocksure in what he believes, and he's a great entertainer—funny and engaging," Jones told me. "He has a beautiful wife and great kids. He's got it all together. There's something to sink your teeth into. He's like any great leader or any great business or ministry. He's a high-competency, high-energy individual. He's just a cut-from-the-cloth leader. People will follow that. It's part of his brilliance."

Jones wants to scratch beneath that cocksure surface and wonders what's really happening with Driscoll. He's suspicious about Driscoll's Reformed convictions. Driscoll didn't have such firm Calvinistic beliefs when they knew each other well. If Driscoll's unflinching confidence attracts some postmoderns, many others chafe at anyone who seems too comfortable with his ability to grasp absolute truth.

"I know conservatism works in the face of globalization," Jones explained. "I don't know if postmodernism works, but I really hope it does. All postmodernism means is living on the shifting sand, as opposed to looking for some foundation. But some of us would say, 'The people who say they stand on the sure foundation—it's not as sure as they think it is. We all live on the slippery slope.'"

But make no mistake, Driscoll seems to have tired of emerging debates about the relationship of theology to postmodernism. Knowing his erstwhile emergent friends will not be persuaded, Driscoll references 641 Bible verses in just fourteen pages of *Listening to the Beliefs of Emerging Churches: Five Perspectives*.[3] Doug Pagitt, pastor of Solomon's Porch in Minneapolis, gets it right when he responds, "I think much of our difference comes from the fact that in many ways we are telling different stories of Christianity."[4]

Such criticism is tame compared to when Driscoll opines about women. Driscoll sustained the most severe criticism of his career in November 2006 due to comments he made after Ted Haggard stepped down as president of the National Association of Evangelicals amid a sex scandal. Writing on his blog, Driscoll offered fellow pastors helpful, practical advice on how to voice sin. But one comment stood out. "It is not uncommon to meet pastors' wives who really let themselves go; they sometimes feel that because their husband is a pastor, he is therefore trapped into fidelity, which gives them cause for laziness," he said. "A wife who lets herself go and is not sexually available to her husband

[3]*Listening to the Beliefs of Emerging Churches: Five Perspectives*, Mark Driscoll, John Burke, Dan Kimball, Doug Pagitt, and Karen Ward, collaborators, ed. Robert Webber (Grand Rapids, MI: Zondervan, 2007), 21–35.
[4]Ibid., 42.

in the ways that the Song of Songs is so frank about is not responsible for her husband's sin, but she may not be helping him either."

Though not directed at Haggard's wife, the comments understandably drew considerable rebuke. A Seattle group called People Against Fundamentalism emerged with plans to picket Mars Hill Church. However, Driscoll preempted the protest by apologizing on his blog and sitting down with its organizers for an extended meeting. Still, Driscoll's church seemed to suffer. Mars Hill fell four hundred thousand dollars behind budget around Christmas, forcing the church to lay off staff for the first time. Then a funny thing happened. Church members, aware of the need, dramatically increased their giving. And in January church attendance grew by one thousand, a 20 percent increase.

Maybe Mars Hill should have expected the growth. Preaching in 2006 about Christ bearing sin on the cross, Driscoll blew out his voice. He had screamed at the church at the top of his lungs for more than an hour during multiple services. Never one to blush, Driscoll bludgeoned the congregation with a graphic description of Jesus' death. He told the church that God hates them in their sin. Many emerging leaders shy away from speaking about penal substitution. They do not believe this way of understanding the atonement connects with postmodern westerners. What sounded normal centuries ago in cultures with animal sacrifice now sounds more like divine child abuse, they argue. Not Driscoll. It's controversial doctrines he pounds hardest.

"I was thinking I'd be meeting in a phone booth next week," Driscoll said about his atonement sermon. "I thought it was over."

Hardly. The next Sunday the church grew by eight hundred.

"The gospel is offensive in an attractive way, and I think in an effort to make the gospel inoffensive we make it unattractive," Driscoll explained. "I mean, the gospel says that you are more evil and wicked than you could ever possibly fathom. But it also says you're more loved and forgiven than you could have ever hoped for. I think we live in an age where everyone's been bought and sold and pitched and marketed, and they just want somebody to get up and tell them the truth and respect their intelligence and let them figure out whether or not they're for it."

This approach differs significantly from emergent churches. For that matter, it differs from the approaches that built today's largest suburban megachurches.

"We're seeker-hostile. We're seeker-insensitive," Driscoll said. "It's like you punch a guy in his face, and he brings his two friends and says, 'Hey, can you punch them too?' It's a weird phenomenon. I'm not going to lie to you."

Given Driscoll's Reformed theology and emerging critique, you might expect that he likes to snipe at boomer megachurches. He did, especially early in his career. Driscoll took some shots at Rick Warren, until Warren wrote him back. But now Driscoll says he appreciates the leading pastor practitioners of church-growth strategies. That might have something to do with the size of his own church. He'll take all the administrative advice he can get from them. The Bible isn't too specific about how to shepherd six thousand church members.

When Driscoll showed up in his office in 2001, Gerry Breshears saw little more than a brash, sarcastic kid who made his mark criticizing boomer churches. Breshears, chair of the division of theological and biblical studies at Western Seminary in Portland, Oregon, also noticed that Driscoll did not lack ambition or vision. Mars Hill, with fifteen hundred members at the time, had plans to grow to twenty thousand.

But Driscoll did lack theological training. That's why he approached Breshears, who has advised Driscoll's studies since then. Once Breshears cut through Driscoll's public persona, he discovered a deep commitment to Scripture and Bible-based theology.

"Since then I've come to realize that Mark is a blinking genius," Breshears said. "He is a first-rank intellect. A lot of his success comes from his amazing intellect and entrepreneurial ability that's one in a million."

That intellect, combined with Driscoll's abrasive style, rubs many the wrong way. Breshears observed that early in Driscoll's career, he took extreme positions just to rattle some cages. The uncertainty of relativism can actually favor those who believe with such firm conviction, even when their teaching cuts against the popular grain. All the better if the leader speaks their language.

"Mark is talking to twenty-somethings, for whom trash talk is their normal language," Breshears observed. "But what he's saying in trash talk is pure Bible."

If Breshears is selling, John MacArthur isn't buying. The venerable expositor appreciates Driscoll's soteriology but finds "his infatuation with the vulgar aspects of contemporary society more disturbing."

The avowed cessationist might be thinking of one particular passage from *Confessions of a Reformission Rev.* "Up to this point I had been basically a theological cessationist and a fan of fundamentalist strawman attacks on charismatic Christians," Driscoll writes. "It wasn't until some years later, however, that I came to see the cessationists' interpretation of 1 Corinthians 12–14 as the second worst exegesis I had ever read, next to that of a Canadian nudist arsonist cult I once did some research on."[5]

Writing in his *Pulpit* magazine, MacArthur leveled against Driscoll possibly the most damning thing you can say about a pastor: "His defense of substitutionary atonement might help his disciples gain a good grasp of the doctrine of justification by faith; but the lifestyle he models—especially his easygoing familiarity with all this world's filthy fads—practically *guarantees* that they will make little progress toward authentic *sanctification*."[6]

MacArthur declined to be interviewed for this book. I asked Driscoll what he made of this criticism.

"It's like a frat guy getting paddled," he responded. "It doesn't feel good, but I guess it means you're in."

Driscoll was effusive in his praise for much of MacArthur's theology and his commitment to inerrancy, expository preaching, and the local church. Driscoll said that as a young Christian he listened to MacArthur's preaching on hundreds of tapes.

"If John MacArthur would have called me or e-mailed me, I would have got on an airplane, flown to Los Angeles, and welcomed his counsel, because I want to do a good job serving Jesus honestly," he told me. "And if somebody who's been serving Jesus faithfully for a long time has some helpful advice, I would welcome it, because I'm on my own.

---

[5]Ibid., 121.
[6]John MacArthur, "Grunge Christianity?" *Pulpit Magazine*, December 11, 2006; http://www.sfpulpit.com/2006/12/11/grunge-christianity/.

I don't have a denomination. I'm just making it up as I go by God's grace."

Though calm in his defense, Driscoll insisted that Seattle's missionary need demands new, creative ways to engage the city with the gospel.

"I'm not a fundamentalist. I don't think they're any fun at all," he said. "I'm a missionary. Fundamentalists avoid culture. Missionaries study it in an effort to reach people. If I were going into China to be a missionary, no one would complain. They wouldn't say, look at that, Mark's wearing Chinese clothes. He's speaking Chinese words. He's listening to Chinese music. Gosh, what is that guy? A liberal? No, he's in China.

"The truth is that Seattle is as lost and pagan as China. And if we're going to send missionaries to China, we have to send missionaries to Seattle. We need to give them the same freedom that we do missionaries in China."

Shifting to offense, Driscoll explained how fundamentalism ensures that the emergent church will have a future.

"Fundamentalism is really losing the war, and it is in part responsible for the rise of what we know as the more liberal end of the emerging church," he said. "Because a lot of what is fueling the left end of the emerging church is fatigue with hard-core fundamentalism that throws rocks at culture. But culture is the house that people live in, and it just seems really mean to keep throwing rocks at somebody's house."

MacArthur has plenty of company among critics who see more pop culture than gospel in Driscoll's leadership. But many of those critics have little in common with MacArthur. Jennifer McKinney directs the women's studies program at Seattle Pacific University. She told me that she started teaching about the sociology of gender in part because of issues raised at Mars Hill Church. After hearing Driscoll debate gender roles in 2003, McKinney left thinking, *If this is Christianity, I want nothing to do with it.*

McKinney and MacArthur sit on opposite ends of the gender-role debate, but they agree that Driscoll's comfort with culture obscures his Bible message.

"You see that kind of hard line in some of these evangelical churches that say the gospel is offensive," McKinney told me in her office. "Well, I don't know that the gospel is offensive. It's counter-cultural. The problem I see is that in trying to be countercultural, what culture are they trying to counter? When you bring in really great rock music and topical sermons, that seems to be edgy. But what I find is that for the most part it's not actually countercultural; it's actually just assimilating to the culture. I think a lot of evangelicals don't recognize that a lot of what happens in the evangelical church is not particularly Christian, but it's particularly American."

But whereas MacArthur worries that Mars Hill members cannot change, McKinney sees all too much change in female students who attend the church.

"I can't say that folks who go to his church are not active, thinking beings, but the perception on campus with some of the women is that they completely change," McKinney said. "Although they wanted to be social workers or they wanted to be youth pastors, now they will say, 'You know what, those aren't appropriate for women, because what God calls us to do is to be good wives and mothers.'"

I repeated the critiques from MacArthur and McKinney to Wendy Alsup, the Mars Hill deacon responsible for women's theology and training. She moved to Seattle from South Carolina along with some friends who wanted to plant a church. The friends went elsewhere, but Alsup opted for Mars Hill, which she found on an Internet search.

"It was very obvious how God didn't need us to tell him about the need for culturally relevant Reformed ministry in Seattle," she said. "He had already known and had been working on that for a couple of years."

Alsup brought along her sleeping infant for our interview in the "war room," where Mars Hill's sizable security detail meets and stores their equipment. It turned out to be an apt location. Alsup, thirty-seven, was plenty familiar with every charge leveled at Driscoll and the women who attend Mars Hill. Only a couple of minutes into our interview, Alsup began trembling with righteous indignation.

"We'll always be open to criticism," she said, "because God has grown us faster than we can handle."

Open to criticism, yes. Happy about it? No.

"We're in the ER after the World Trade Center here at Mars Hill," said Alsup, shaking. "We don't have ten people with big problems because they just got saved last week. We've got a thousand. And we are running to disciple them, to minister the Word to them, to teach them the gospel. If you're not going to come and help us, at least stop throwing rocks at our windows while we're trying to treat our patients."

With so many critics ready to pounce on Driscoll, I was surprised to hear Robert Wall offer complimentary words. Wall teaches Scripture and Wesleyan studies at Seattle Pacific University, an evangelical school just minutes away from Mars Hill. Wall and Driscoll packed the nearby Free Methodist church in 2003 to debate gender roles. They don't see eye-to-eye on this and other important matters. Speaking to me in his office, Wall agreed that Driscoll has earned his reputation as loud and brash. But he offered Driscoll high praise for training his church to think theologically. That's something Wall has learned to appreciate, even from a Calvinist.

"I think catechesis is the wave of the future," Wall said. "We have to have pastors invested in the theological formation of their congregations or we're lost as a church."

With theology, sometimes you don't know what you have until it's gone. Scott Golike reminded me about this lesson when we talked at the Acts 29 dessert and drinks reception. Golike, fifty-two, has served as a pastor in the Seattle area off and on for more than two decades. Now he is the teaching pastor at Grace Fellowship of Puget Sound, part of the Acts 29 Network. He showed me how Driscoll's influence has broadened beyond young Seattle hipsters. Before planting Grace Fellowship, Golike and his family attended a seeker-sensitive suburban church. The elders observed his pastoral gifts and asked him to join their leadership board. Golike expressed his concern about some church values—namely, an uncertain commitment to theological education. Nevertheless, the elders insisted that he could help them by exercising his unique, needed gifts.

As providence would have it, that same night the pastor told the elder board that he planned to implement Rick Warren's Purpose Driven model. When he did, the church's theological commitment deteriorated even more. The pastor eliminated those supposed barriers that he feared would discourage visitors. It was more than Golike could take.

"If you make everything about the unchurched," Golike said, "no matter what else you say and do, you really fall short of building the body."

Driscoll's Reformed convictions drew Golike to Acts 29. At the boot camp I attended, Golike served as an evaluator. He estimated that only about 25 percent of the men who attend boot camps get the full seal of approval for Acts 29. Recognizing the difficulty of planting a church, Acts 29 thoroughly evaluates candidates. The network, now with nearly one hundred churches in the United States and others around the world, also requires member pastors and churches to agree on certain beliefs, such as Reformed soteriology and male elders. But Acts 29 churches exercise discretion on how to reach their unique local contexts. Network leaders have set a goal of planting one thousand new churches in the next twenty years. Another ministry outgrowth of Mars Hill, The Resurgence, trains churches to be "culturally accessible and biblically faithful."

This combination is the strength of Driscoll's ministry, according to Golike. Healthy churches will excel at both. He appreciates that seeker-sensitive churches picked up the evangelism slack where many traditional churches failed. Starting his church, Golike decided to own the criticism that so-called notebook Christians can get fat and content with Bible and doctrine. Golike refused to compromise in-depth expositional preaching, but he knew the church would need a specific strategy for evangelism. They couldn't just talk about evangelism and hope it would happen. He sees great promise in the missional approach because church members share the mission to take the gospel outside church walls. Men who like softball play in city leagues. Women who like stamping join clubs. Well, not at Mars Hill. But missional Christianity in Golike's suburban church will not look like Mars Hill. And that's okay with Driscoll. What matters is the mission, he writes in *The Radical Reformission: Reaching Out Without Selling Out.*

He says, "God's mission is not to create a team of moral and decent people but rather to create a movement of holy loving missionaries who are comfortable and truthful around lost sinners and who, in this way, look more like Jesus than most of his pastors do."[7]

After the boot camp I stuck around Mars Hill for a Sunday service. I arrived about forty-five minutes early on Sunday morning to make sure I could nab a parking spot. The church's main campus is a former Napa Auto Parts store in Ballard. The simple, spacious building seats twelve hundred in a dark auditorium but still reserves abundant space elsewhere for nurseries.

Anticipation began building about half an hour before the 9 A.M. service started. College students and other young adults quickly surrounded me and saved seats up front for their friends. The whole setting felt like a rock concert—surely the church's intent. Two bouncers flanked either end of the stage. Biceps folded and flaunted with tight black T-shirts, they stared down the congregation. Earpieces connected them with Mars Hill's extensive security presence. Just inside the church entrance to the left you can see the "war room." It all seems a bit much, until you hear the stories. Last fall a man wielding a knife stormed the stage. Security sacked him before he could reach Driscoll.

At least on this day the security may not have been needed. Driscoll did not even preach. He opened his pulpit to Bruce Ware, professor of systematic theology at Southern Baptist Theological Seminary. Ware preached for sixty-five minutes on God's self-sufficiency. Driscoll typically preaches at least that long.

Ware had flown out to Seattle to lead a Resurgence conference. Beginning Friday night and concluding Saturday afternoon, Ware delivered three ninety-minute lectures on seminary-level systematic theology. He covered four models of God's providence—process theology, open theism, Arminianism, and Calvinism. The conference drew more than four hundred young adults, most of them from the host church. As Ware taught, I couldn't help but think that rumors of systematic theology's demise have been greatly exaggerated. If New Testament scholar Scot McKnight is correct, Driscoll no longer seems to have a home in the emerging church.

---

[7]Mark Driscoll, *The Radical Reformission: Reaching Out Without Selling Out* (Grand Rapids, MI: Zondervan, 2004), 35.

"The emerging movement tends to be suspicious of systematic theology," McKnight wrote in *Christianity Today*. "Why? Not because we don't read systematics, but because the diversity of theologies alarms us, no genuine consensus has been achieved, God didn't reveal a systematic theology but a storied narrative, and no language is capable of capturing the Absolute Truth who alone is God."[8]

Lynette Palmer drove from Spokane, Washington, to attend the Resurgence conference. She graciously introduced herself before the Sunday morning service began. I think she interpreted my "awkward journalist" vibe to guess I was an awkward visitor.

Lynette, twenty-five, told me that systematic theology fills a generational need. "Our generation has grown up in a culture all about the self," she said. "But the self focus isn't feeding our hearts. We have great need for systematic theology. A lot of churches aren't teaching it."

Lynette spent time in a charismatic church with no strong theological bent after she became a Christian at the University of Washington through Campus Crusade. Theology is no mere hobby or matter of semantics for Lynette. Life has dealt her family a wretched hand. In the last few years her mother and three sisters have come to faith. But her father spent eight years in jail—for raping one of Lynette's sisters.

"When I first became a Christian, before I had a good theological foundation, I saw the abuse as something that was apart from God," Lynette said. "It was evil, and God is good. And so it was probably what Satan wanted and not what God wanted."

Her evolving view of God's sovereignty changed everything. By appearances, her father's sin destroyed her sister. But Lynette understood that God would never leave or forsake her sister. Rather he would ensure her perseverance. In God's sovereign plan, even the horrific abuse she suffered would somehow work to the good. No matter how awful the pain, Satan could not defeat her.

As Lynette counseled her sister, Reformed theology provided a foundation and understanding of God's sovereignty that could empower them to transcend these circumstances. I could hardly believe the tremendous faith Lynette exhibited as she told me about their

---

[8]Scot McKnight, "Five Streams of the Emerging Church," *Christianity Today*, February 2007, 38.

troubles. God set her free from suffering and pain when she understood what Scripture teaches about God's authority.

Lynette works for a Spokane ministry called Cup of Cold Water, which helps homeless teenagers. She also volunteers with Young Life and Campus Crusade. She told me that Reformed theology emboldens her ministry.

"Working with homeless teenagers, I would leave crying because I could see Satan's hand around them and pulling them out of the picture," she explained. "I was giving Satan more authority and power than he has. And once I started getting a foundation and looking at what God says about his sovereignty, I realized that Satan has no power to destroy people."

Lynette's story reminded me about what Driscoll had said a couple of days earlier.

"I believe that doctrine is not just true; I also believe it's helpful. In addition to arguing for the truth of the doctrine, we also need to show the helpfulness of the doctrine," he told me. "At its best, the historical stream of Reformed theology is really for people in life."

Reformed theology runs afoul when zealous activists would rather score debate points than worship God with holy lives and love for their neighbors. At its best, Calvinism makes a difference. Transcendence doesn't just give Christians an excuse to sing songs that mention "glory" in every other verse. The transcendent God inspires fear and trembling. He demands holiness, but not without offering his Son as a sacrifice for our sins and sending his Holy Spirit to comfort us. Scripture refuses to condone any response but humility.

And as it did for the apostle Paul, humility should engender action. God goes before us. What greater comfort in evangelism could there be, what greater hope for social justice?

"The guys who read Paul and want to fight for his doctrine should have an equal amount of zeal to follow in his example," Driscoll said. "A lot of Calvinists talk like Paul; they don't act like him."

By their fruit, Calvinists will thrive or decline once again.

Epilogue

Fog lingered over the rolling countryside as I drove past familiar terrain. The previous day's rain had rejuvenated the endless fields of deep-green
soybeans and golden-tasseled corn. That's critical news for small prairie towns
like Dell Rapids, dependent on the fruit of the land that surrounds them. I
pulled into the South Dakota hamlet on Sunday morning and rolled toward
downtown, past the Dairy Queen and two funeral homes. Dell Rapids boasts a
historic downtown, with storefronts more than one hundred years old chiseled
from red stone mined in a nearby quarry. Visiting the town as a child, I cared
less about history than I did the buffet at Pizza Ranch, across the street from the
historical society and next to the newspaper.

But Dell Rapids has changed a fair bit since my childhood. For one thing,
the pizza joint vacated its downtown site. These days it's hard for businesses
to survive in South Dakota's isolated villages. Nevertheless, downtown buzzed
with activity as I arrived. Even on Sunday morning I struggled to find a parking spot. Everyone was heading for the same place, the space vacated by Pizza
Ranch. That's the new home of River Community Church, planted in February
2006 and part of the North American Baptist Conference.

I discovered River Community Church while searching on the 9Marks web
site for churches in my native South Dakota. 9Marks takes its name from Mark
Dever's book *Nine Marks of a Healthy Church* and runs out of offices in Capitol
Hill Baptist Church. Imagine my surprise when I learned that the pastor who
planted River Community Church had been a high-school friend. Andy Wright
was a student leader in the ministry God used to reach me. I remembered Andy
as a responsible, kind, soft-spoken teenager. But the pastor who met me at the
door looked like he could have led a church in the Acts 29 Network. His shaved
head accentuated angular features. He left a vertical-striped, button-down shirt
untucked over dark-olive cargo pants. Only the Scandinavian "o" in his accent
betrayed his rural plains upbringing.

After a few rounds of genial chitchat, the small church crowd, about fifty
strong, got up from leather couches in the foyer and leisurely moved into the

sanctuary. The decor looked more like Mars Hill Church than any other site I had visited. The newly painted walls alternated between olive and burnt orange. Families sat down around tables as the small guitar-driven worship ensemble took their places. Seemingly half the congregation cleared out when elementary-age children were invited to join their own program. During the opening announcements, church leaders recruited babysitters for an upcoming community outreach. The music took cues from Passion, highlighted by Matt Redman's "Blessed Be Your Name." The choice of song, which encourages praise in good and bad circumstances, could not have been a coincidence. Andy, twenty-seven, preached from Psalm 63 and recounted David's severe family problems. He exhorted the congregation to persevere through troubles and to ask God for a transformed heart, the conduit to greater faith, greater worship, greater passion, and a greater understanding of God's Word. "God's glory satisfies us," Andy told them. God's love should enrapture and ravish our hearts, he said. "Let your heart burn inside for God." Toward this end, he encouraged the crowd to read great books. He recommended *The Life and Diary of David Brainerd*, culled from the journals of the missionary who died in the home of Jonathan Edwards. Half. com sells used copies for only four dollars, he assured them.

After the service I joined Andy and a small group for lunch. It turns out that the Pizza Ranch is alive and well. You have to head toward the brand-new restaurant on the town's outskirts if you want the delicious lunch buffet. Dell Rapids has actually experienced a fair amount of growth in recent years. New homes surround the golf course. Historically reliant on farms and the rock quarry, Dell Rapids has become a bedroom community for Sioux Falls, not more than twenty minutes away down Interstate 29. Many parents commute to Sioux Falls to work for credit-card companies, hospitals, and ethanol producers but prefer to raise their families in small towns. The bright future for Dell Rapids helped Andy decide to plant his family and his church there.

After Andy drove me around town on a tour, we settled down in Dairy Queen to talk about the growing allure of Reformed theology and challenges of church planting. We talked about the difficulty of starting an evangelical church in a community dominated by Lutherans and Roman Catholics. In the same town where evangelical churches prompt murmurs of cult activity, two bikers walked into Dairy Queen wearing leather jackets with Servants for Christ and Set Free etched on the back. A couple of minutes later a woman walked in the door wearing a campaign T-shirt for the state representative who led an effort to ban abortion.

Andy grew up in an evangelical church. He attended a North American

Baptist church a few blocks away from the United Methodist church of my youth. Despite graduating high school in a class of only nine students, he headed to Chicago for college at Moody Bible Institute. At Moody, Andy invested great energy into fighting Calvinists. Apparently he didn't win those debates.

"Once you start seeing Reformed theology in Scripture, you realize it's all over the place," he said. "It's like there's a big revolution in your mind. Stuff that didn't make sense before starts to make sense. It's been an incredible journey, and it's increased my passion for God."

Other students and a couple of professors introduced him to John Piper. He was gripped by Piper's submission to Scripture and enthusiasm for missions. It's evident that Andy has patterned his ministry after Piper. He has taken 2 Corinthians 3:18 as a theme verse.

"My preaching isn't about moralistic dos and don'ts," Andy said. "I want to show God to people. Beholding God's glory transforms them. I just want to point them in that direction. Without preaching moralism, you see better morals."

Much to my surprise, I learned that Andy now has plenty of like-minded company among area pastors. Andy recruited a group of five other pastors and seminary students to meet me in a Sioux Falls coffee shop and talk Reformed theology. Before planting the church in Dell Rapids, Andy worked with youth at Central Valley Community Church in nearby Hartford, another Sioux Falls bedroom community. Chris Gorman, the pastor who planted that church in 2000, once helped lead the student ministry that nurtured Andy and me. At his church's outset, Chris, thirty-four, took his cues from the seeker-sensitive megachurches. Sure enough, the church grew. But after only a couple of years Chris felt like he was running out of steam. He nearly burned out trying to top the previous week's drama, video interviews, dynamic music, and topical sermon. Andy began to talk to him about Reformed theology. Once Chris got past the labels and into the Scriptures, his guard fell. Chris even preached limited atonement from John 3:16.

"I felt free for the first time," Chris said. "I saw hard passages as good. I felt like I was saved again for the first time."

The church had a somewhat harder time adjusting. He led an adult Sunday school class through *The Blazing Center*, a DVD teaching series by Piper. The class complained to Chris that the material flew over their heads. Many preferred the 40 Days of Purpose campaign he had led a couple of years earlier. Then Chris tried the Piper DVDs on the youth. They had no problem following Piper, he said.

Still, that's nothing compared to what Ryan Franchuk teaches the youth at First Baptist Church in Emery, South Dakota, population four hundred and fifty. He handed me a ten-page, self-published booklet called "The Handy-Dandy Doctrines of Grace Bible Verse Reference Guide." Ryan's list of proof texts on TULIP is now in its fifth edition. During Sunday school, he teaches the youth a modified version of the Millard Erickson and Louis Berkhof systematic theologies.

"They grab on like you wouldn't believe," said Ryan, twenty-eight. "It's almost like a second conversion. They talk about going to far-off lands and dying for the gospel."

For nearly two years, I traveled across the country and talked with the leading pastors and theologians of the growing Reformed movement. I sat in John Piper's den, Al Mohler's office, C. J. Mahaney's church, and Jonathan Edwards's college. But the backbone of the Reformed resurgence comprises ordinary churches like those I saw in South Dakota—churches used by God to do extraordinary things. Armed with God's Word and transformed by the Holy Spirit, these churches' leaders faithfully proclaim the gospel of Jesus Christ week after week, through tragedy and triumph. Culture has conspired to give their message a wider audience. Desire for transcendence and tradition among young evangelicals has contributed to a Reformed resurgence.

One of Ryan Franchuk's students, near the beginning of high school, asked him if he could get into Scripture without having to read it. Taken aback, Ryan sheepishly recommended audio Bibles. But just three years later the student brought *The Life of David Brainerd* to camp. Now he weeps for the lost. He asked Ryan to teach him Greek basics so he could better understand the New Testament. He wants to serve as a missionary to unreached people groups.

Hunger for God's Word. Passion for evangelism. Zeal for holiness. That's not a revival of Calvinism. That's a revival. And it's breaking out in places like Emery, South Dakota.

Index